**FOOLS & KINGS, D.E.M.
AND THEATRE503
PRESENT**

CLICKBAIT

BY MILLY THOMAS

Clickbait was developed and produced by Fools & Kings,
D.E.M. Productions and Theatre503, and received its world premiere
at Theatre503 on Tuesday 19 January 2016

CAST

Nicola Georgia Groome

Gina Amy Dunne

Chloe Alice Hewkin

Adam/Promoter Barney White

Kat Emma D'Arcy

CREATIVE TEAM

Director Holly Race Roughan

Designer Frankie Bradshaw

Lighting Designer Matthew Swithinbank

Sound Designer Max Perryment

Movement Director Katie Payne

Associate Director Thomas Bailey

Design Assistant Isobel Pellow

PRODUCTION TEAM

Producers Jessica Campbell, Jack Sain & Ramin Sabi

Associate Producer Ceri Lothian

Production Manager James Ashby

Stage Manager Rike Berg

Production PR Chloe Nelkin Consulting

CAST

GEORGIA GROOME (NICOLA)

Georgia is best known for her lead role in Gurinder Chadha's *Angus, Thongs and Perfect Snogging*. Her other film credits include *Taking Stock*, *The Holding* and *London to Brighton*. Her television credits include *Up The Women* (BBC); *The Bright Side* (BBC) and *Lewis* (ITV). Her stage work includes *Tutto Bene Mamma* (The Print Room) and *Tusk, Tusk* (Royal Court).

AMY DUNN (GINA)

Amy's credits include *Chatroom* (Arcola/C Nova); *Happy* (Pleasance Dome); *The Vortex* (Bridewell Theatre); and *The Graduate* (Courtyard Theatre). Her television credits include *Dickensian* (BBC) and *The Tracey Ullman Sketch Show* (BBC). Her radio credits include *His Dark Materials* (BBC). Amy has just graduated from Royal Central School of Speech and Drama, where her credits included *The Low Road*, *The Priory*, *Angels in America*, *The Oresteia* and *Romeo & Juliet*.

ALICE HEWKIN (CHLOE)

Alice's stage credits include *Hidden* (Royal Court); *The Vote* (Donmar Warehouse) and *To Avoid Precipice Cling to Rock* (Bedlam Theatre). Her television credits include *Cuckoo* (BBC); *Fishbowl* (BBC); *The Vote* (Channel 4); *The Bakerstreet Irregulars* (BBC); *Stella* (Sky); *Doctors* (BBC) *Teacup Travels* (CBBC) *Game of Thrones* (HBO) and *Japanese Samurai Sword* (Short film: BAFTA Screening). Alice trained at Central, where her credits included *Twelfth Night*, *The Seagull*, *Hamlet* and *Tartuffe*.

BARNEY WHITE (ADAM/PROMOTER)

Barney's film credits include *Testament of Youth* (Heyday Films) and *Social Suicide*. His television credits include *The Musketeers* (BBC) and *Holby City* (BBC).

EMMA D'ARCY (KAT)

Emma D'Arcy's credits include *Romeo and Juliet* (Tokyo Met/Saitama Arts/Southwark Playhouse/Yvonne Arnaud); *The Pillowman* (Oxford Playhouse); *Bunny* (BT Studio); *The Comedy of Errors* (Tokyo Met/Southwark Playhouse/Yvonne Arnaud); *The Caucasian Chalk Circle* (Oxford Playhouse); *The Cosmonaut's Last Message...* (O'Reilly Theatre) and devised production *Grimm* (C-too, Edinburgh). Emma co-founded and coordinated forum theatre project 'Act for Change: Cameroon', and in 2016 will be Artistic Director of *Callisto: a queer epic* by Howard Coase.

CREATIVES

MILLY THOMAS [WRITER]

Milly Thomas is a writer and actor. She graduated from the BA Acting course at the Royal Central School of Speech and Drama in 2014, where she began writing alongside acting. Her first full-length play *A First World Problem* opened at Theatre503 in July 2014 to critical acclaim. Her second play *Piggies* was commissioned in 2015 by the Royal Central School of Speech and Drama. She joined the Young Writers' Lab at Soho Theatre in 2014 and is a member of 'Headstart' – a group comprising of ten playwrights assembled by Headlong Theatre Company alongside Blacklisted Films. She has taken part in writers' rooms for Pure Grass Films and Balloon Entertainment and has been selected for the 2016 Channel 4 Screenwriting Course. She is currently writing an episode of the BBC3 series *Clique* which is set to air in 2017.

HOLLY RACE ROUGHAN [DIRECTOR]

Holly trained in Theatre Directing at Birkbeck College. She is Associate Director on the National Theatre's & Headlong's *People, Places and Things* in the West End. Credits as Director include *No One Will Tell Me How to Start a Revolution* (R&D – RSC); *The Low Road* (The Embassy Theatre – CSSD); *Animal* (The Gate – RWCMD); *Eye of a Needle* (Southwark Playhouse); *A First World Problem* (Theatre503); *Pages From My Songbook* (Royal Exchange Studio, Manchester); *Believers Anonymous* (Rosemary Branch); *Waiting For Alice* (Pleasance – Edinburgh Fringe Festival); *After the War* (Cambridge ADC). As Staff Director/Assistant Director: *The Shoemaker's Holiday* (RSC); *Hotel* (National Theatre); *The Pass* (Royal Court); *Three Birds* (Bush Theatre/Royal Exchange); *The Birthday Party*, *A Doll's House*, *Rat's Tales* and *The Country Wife* (Royal Exchange). Holly also directs original dramas in prison for the charity Kestrel.

FRANKIE BRADSHAW [DESIGNER]

Frankie Bradshaw completed an Art Foundation Course at Wimbledon College of Art, before studying BA Theatre and Performance Design at Liverpool Institute for Performing Arts, graduating with first class honors. She was a Linbury Prize finalist in 2015 for her work with the Lyric, Belfast. Since graduating she has worked as costume designer for *Barbarians* (Young Vic); and as set and costume designer for *Brink* (Royal Exchange Studio, Manchester); *Grav* (Torch Theatre, Wales and touring); *A First World Problem* (Theatre 503); and *Stories from the Sea* (Unity Theatre, Liverpool). Frankie has also worked as design assistant to Christopher Oram on a number of productions including *Man and Superman* (National Theatre); *A Damsel in Distress* (Chichester Festival Theatre); *Photograph 51* (Noel Coward Theatre); and is associate designer on the Kenneth Branagh Theatre Company season at the Garrick theatre.

MATTHEW SWITHINBANK (LIGHTING DESIGNER)

Matthew is a London-based lighting designer and technician from Luxembourg. Having studied Technical Theatre at Mountview Academy of Theatre Arts, he now works as a technician and lighting designer throughout London, as well as on tour. Credits include *Fugee & Wasted* (Southwark Playhouse); *Game Theory* (Tristan Bates); *A First World Problem* (Theatre503); *Warehouse of Dreams* (Lion and Unicorn); *Safe Sex & On Tidy Endings* (Tristan Bates); *There Is A War* (Jackson's Lane); *Victor Frankenstein* (King's Arms, Salford); *White Rose* & *Very Pleasant Sensations* (Cockpit); *Jane Eyre* (Mierscher Kulturhaus & Abbaye Neumunster, Luxembourg); and *The Devil His Due* (FEATS2011, Geneva).

MAX PERRYMENT (SOUND DESIGNER)

Max Perryment is a composer and sound designer. He has composed extensively for commericials and TV adverts. His most recent work for theatre includes *Creditors, The Remarkable Case of K.* and *The Surplus* (Young Vic Theatre); *Sense of an Ending,* (Theatre 503); *And Then Come the Nightjars,* (Theatre 503 and Bristol Old Vic); *Three Lions* (St James' Theatre and tour) and *Black Dog Gold Fish* (The Vaults Festival). He was recently nominated for an Offie and a Broadway World Award for Best Sound Design.

KATIE PAYNE (MOVEMENT DIRECTOR)

Katie collaborated with director Holly Race Roughan on *Eye Of A Needle* (Southwark Playhouse), *A First World Problem* (Theatre503), *The Low Road* (CSSD) and *No One Will Tell Me How To Start A Revolution* (RSC). She has worked with physical theatre company Frantic Assembly as a movement director on *Little Dogs* (National Theatre of Wales) and as a performer in *The Curious Incident of The Dog In The Night-Time* (National Theatre and West-End Apollo Theatre). Other credits as an actor include *'Tis Pity She's A Whore* (RSC Players), *Presas* (Soho Theatre), *Maximillien's Journey* (Jermyn Street Theatre). Through both performing and choreography, she has always been interested in how movement, music and text reflect contemporary culture.

THOMAS BAILEY (ASSOCIATE DIRECTOR)

Thomas Bailey has trained with National Youth Theatre, Cardboard Citizens and Living Pictures. His directing credits include: *Romeo and Juliet* (OUDS International Tour 2015); *A Town Called Freedom* (North Wall Arts Theatre); *The Pillowman* (Oxford Playhouse) and *Devised Play One: Fear* (Burton Taylor Studio). As assistant/associate: *These are your lives* (The Yard Theatre); *The Cosmonaut's Last Message...* (O'Reilly). As writer and director *The Tragedie of MacClegg* (Paradise, Edinburgh). He founded and coordinated forum theatre project 'Act For Change: Cameroon'. This year, Thomas will be directing *Callisto: a queer epic* by Howard Coase, *Children and Animals* by Florence Read, and co-directing a new translation of Brecht's unfinished play *Fatzer*.

ISOBEL PELLOW (DESIGN ASSISTANT)

Isobel has worked on costume design for various theatres in London, the Ashcroft Theatre, the Old Red Lion, English Touring Opera and The Place. She is working as a costume assistant on *Four Play* (Theatre503). Prior to this, Isobel designed costumes for the Oxford Playhouse and the Old Fire Station, Oxford. Isobel initially studied at Warwick University, during which time she got involved in costume with various companies in the area, including the Loft Theatre in Leamington Spa.

JAMES ASHBY (PRODUCTION MANAGER)

James trained at East 15 Acting School, studying carpentry as his major. He now works for The Scenery Shop as Production Carpenter, where his credits include *4000 Days* (Park Theatre) and *The Den* (The Hive, Hackney). Production Management credits include: *Treasure* (The Finborough Theatre); *Sense of an Ending* (Theatre503); *Donkey Heart* (Trafalgar Studios); *The Njogel Opera* (Tête à tête Opera Festival) and Assistant Production Manager on *The Little Green Swallow* (The Peacock Theatre.)

RIKE BERG (STAGE MANAGER)

Rike graduated from the Bauhaus University Weimar in Germany, and has worked on various theatre productions in Sweden and the UK. Her most recent credits as Stage Manager / Assistant Stage Manager include: *The Woman in Black* (Gothenburg English Studio Theatre and Sweden Tour); *Belongings* (GEST); *Upper Cut* (Southwark Playhouse); *Sense of an Ending* (Theatre 503) and *Lines* (The Yard Theatre). Since moving to London Rike has also worked for the Pleasance London, the Gate Theatre, the Bush Theatre and the Royal Albert Hall.

DEUS EX MACHINA PRODUCTIONS (PRODUCER)

DEM Productions was set up by producers Jessica Campbell and Ramin Sabi to produce high quality plays in London's Off West End. They have produced seven productions, which have accrued 9 OffWestEnd Award, 6 BroadwayWorld Award nominations, and 48 ★★★★ or ★★★★★reviews between them.

DEM Productions include: *How I Learned To Drive* and *A Bright Room Called Day* (Southwark Playhouse); *Sense of an Ending* and *First World Problem* (Theatre503); *Stink Foot* at (The Yard Theatre); *Donkey Heart* (Trafalgar Studios) and *Piranha Heights* (Old Red Lion).

Jessica is the in-house Producer & Head of Marketing at Theatre503 where she has produced *And Then Come the Nightjars* (also at Bristol Old Vic) and *Valhalla*. She has worked for James Seabright Productions and Old Vic New Voices.

Ramin has recently co-produced *Gypsy* starring Imelda Staunton (Savoy Theatre, West End); *Let It Be* (Garrick Theatre); and *Annie* (UK & Ireland Tour). He is also producer and CFO for Zoya Films where he has produced a number of commercials, short films and music videos. He is currently executive producer on an independent feature film 'Butterfly Kisses'

FOOLS & KINGS (PRODUCER)

Jack Sain trained at LAMDA and his credits as a director include *Four Play* (Old Vic New Voices); *How I Learned To Drive* (Southwark Playhouse); *That's the Spirit!* (RWR, Theatre503*); Angels in America* (Oxford Playhouse); *Machinal* (Oxford Castle, C Venues, Arcola) and *Cymbeline* (Tabard). His credits as a producer include *Robbie Wakes* and *Mr Kolpert* (Edinburgh Fringe) and *Oleanna* (Tristan Bates). He is the new Resident Assistant Director at the Donmar Warehouse, where his upcoming assisting includes *Welcome Home, Captain Fox!* (dir. Blanche McIntyre); *Elegy* (dir. Josie Rourke) and *Faith Healer* (dir. Lyndsey Turner). He also works as a photographer.

CERI LOTHIAN (ASSOCIATE PRODUCER)

Ceri graduated from The University of Kent with a First class honours degree in Drama and English Literature in July 2015. She worked as Resident Assistant Producer at Theatre503 from May–November 2015, and was on the producing team for the inaugural Theatre503 Award Season plays *And Then Come The Nightjars* and *Valhalla*. Other producing credits whilst studying include *Cabaret* (Gulbenkian Theatre); *Bad* (Colyer-Fergusson Music Hall) and *Spring Awakening* (Marlowe Theatre Studio).

THANKS

Alex Ferris at Old Vic New Voices
Bryony Corrigan
Cordelia Lynn
Deirde O'Halloran
Donmar Warehouse
Ella Thomas
Emily Russell and the Art Academy
James and Nicole Jansz
Jerwood Space
Jules Haworth
Jung Hwa Capon
Lisa Cagnacci
Lora Hristova
Neil and Julia Thomas
Nicola Wren
PwC
Sam Woolf
Sara, Robbie and Alex Lowenstein
Serena Jennings
Soho Theatre
The Young Vic
Tom Hackley at Have Sound
Trevor Simon-Spooner

SUBSIDISED REHEARSAL FACILITIES PROVIDED BY

JERWOOD SPACE

THEATRE503 IS THE AWARD-WINNING HOME OF GROUNDBREAKING PLAYS

Led by Artistic Director Paul Robinson, Theatre503 is a flagship fringe venue committed to producing new work that is game-changing, relevant, surprising, mischievous, visually thrilling and theatrical. We are the smallest theatre to win an Olivier award and we offer more opportunities to new writers than anywhere in the UK.

THEATRE503 TEAM

Artistic Director – Paul Robinson
Executive Director – Jeremy Woodhouse
Producer and Head of Marketing – Jessica Campbell
Associate Artistic Director – Lisa Cagnacci
Literary Manager – Steve Harper
Literary Coordinators – Lauretta Barrow, Tom Latter
Office Manager – Anna De Freitas
Resident Assistant Producers – Scott Barnett, Jack Paterson
Theatre503 Intern – Sam Read
'Young Creative Leaders' Project Manager – Louise Abbots
Volunteer Coordinators – Serafina Cusack, Simon Mander
Associate Directors – Anna Jordan, Jonathan O'Boyle
Senior Readers – Karis Halsall, Kate Brower, Clare O'Hara,
Jimmy Osbourne, Imogen Sarre

THEATRE503 BOARD

Royce Bell, Peter Benson, Chris Campbell, Kay Ellen Consolver, Ben Hall, Dennis Kelly, Eleanor Lloyd, Marcus Markou, Geraldine Sharpe-Newton, Jack Tilbury, Erica Whyman (Chair), Roy Williams.

We couldn't do what we do without out brilliant volunteers:

Andrei Vornicu, Annabel Pemberton, Bethany Doherty, Charlotte Mulliner, Chidi Chukwu, Damian Robertson, Danielle Wilson, Fabienne Gould, George Linfield, James Hansen, Joanna Lallay, Kelly Agredo, Ken Hawes, Larner Taylor, Mandy Nicholls, Mark Doherty, Mike Murgaz, Nicole Marie, Rahim Dhanji, Rosie Akerman, Tess Hardy.

Theatre503 is supported by:

Philip and Chris Carne, Cas Donald, Gregory Dunlop, Angela Hyde-Courtney and the Audience Club, Stephanie Knauf, Sumintra Latchman, Katherine Malcom, Georgia Oetker, Francesca Ortona, Geraldine Sharpe-Newton.

Support Theatre503

Help us take risks on new writers and produce the plays other theatres can't, or won't. Together we can discover the writers of tomorrow and make some of the most exciting theatre in the country. With memberships ranging from £23 to £1003 there is a chance to get involved no matter what your budget, to help us remain *arguably the most important theatre in Britain today'* (*The Guardian*).

Benefits range from priority notice of our work and news, access to sold out shows, ticket deals, and opportunities to attend parties and peek into rehearsals. Visit theatre503.com or call 020 7978 7040 for more details.

CLICKBAIT

Milly Thomas

CLICKBAIT

OBERON BOOKS
LONDON

WWW.OBERONBOOKS.COM

First published in 2016 by Oberon Books Ltd
521 Caledonian Road, London N7 9RH
Tel: +44 (0) 20 7607 3637 / Fax: +44 (0) 20 7607 3629
e-mail: info@oberonbooks.com
www.oberonbooks.com

A catalogue record for this book is available from the British
Library.

PB ISBN: 9781783197224
E ISBN: 9781783197231

Cover design by Jack Sain

Printed, bound and converted
by CPI Group (UK) Ltd, Croydon, CR0 4YY.

Characters

GINA	KAT
The oldest sister	The same age as Nicola
NICOLA	TROLLS
The middle sister	
	JOURNALISTS
CHLOE	
The youngest sister	POLICEMAN
	POLICEWOMAN
ADAM	
The same age as Nicola	PROMOTER

Notes on the play

The play should be performed with movement and sound.

The play spans six years.

The set may be as detailed or as abstract as is desired.

The Trolls/Journalists may be physically performed by the company or presented as voice over.

Cultural references in the text may be updated for future performances where relevant.

Notes on the text

/ Indicates an overlap in dialogue.

// Indicates simultaneous speech.

– Indicates an interruption.

… Indicates a trailing off or searching for words except for when it is used alone when it indicates a desire to speak.

Commas have been used for grammatical purposes and need not be adhered to in performance.

This text went to press before the end of rehearsals so may differ to the final performance.

For Holly

PROLOGUE

We are in an auditorium.

Applause. NICOLA takes to the stage.

NICOLA: Thank you. Thank you all for coming. No pun intended. And thank you to those who are watching from home. Welcome.

(Beat.) I'd like to start by saying that I identify as feminist. For the record, for you all, for posterity, for women: I am a feminist.

I find it disheartening that the nature of what I do has resulted in my feminism being placed under sharp focus. To accuse me of being antifeminist is intrinsically antifeminist. Feminism is unwell. It is ailing. Feminism is refusing to see a doctor. There is something rotten in the state of sisterhood. And my sisters and I are going to flush it out.

Now, it is no great reveal to any of you how we came to be here. How my sisters and I arrived in this industry. How I became 'Nicola Barker'. And to lie in bed cumming repeatedly would be far easier than becoming CEO of the most exciting pornographic start-up in Europe, I can tell you.

Laughter.

But I've got ahead of myself.

Silence.

I'm here today because my sisters and I have created something special. We have created a way. A booth. A home movie booth – if you like. A home from home. A capitalisation of the amateur porn market.

Welcome to 'Protest' – the first female led, family-run sex business that has no links to prostitution. Go professional. Test your limits. This is not a service we are providing. We are creating the conditions for you to provide a much-deserved and much-needed service to yourselves.

Revenge pornography will slowly become redundant. Why? Because there will be no shame. There will be No Judgement. Post away. Your videos will not hurt us. They will celebrate us. You are giving us a thumbs up. A 'like'. A 'favourite'. We will take the stigma and spread it so thinly that there will be no more exploitation. We will be choosing to 'exploit' ourselves.

My single greatest goal as a business woman won't be to go international. It won't be having celebrities endorse the booths on twitter. It won't be about awards. It will be you. The public.

The ordinary men and women of this world who keep it turning, the nurses, the ticket officers, the teachers, the dog-walkers, the construction workers. The unsung heroes of the world.

There is a porn star in all of you. Male and female. I have closed the gap between the consumer and the consumed to give the public the gift of their inner porn star.

These booths are for fun. They are for healthy sexual activity.

But they are also for love. They are for family. They are for friends. It is bizarre to me that the same process which creates a physical family is so far removed from the sex industry.

Women are sexual creatures. As are men. Those titties you suck on also make milk. These booths celebrate the range of human experience. The same man who loves watching Frozen with his daughter also loves pissing down girls throats. And that is to be celebrated.

Our booths are safe. They are hygienic. They are friendly. They are warm. They were created out of a deep emotional bond and understanding. They were created out of love. Which, as sisters, we have in spades.

My name is Nicola Barker. And I am a feminist.

Go professional. Test your limits.

There will be No Judgement.

Thank you.

Applause. During the applause NICOLA puts on pyjamas. The sounds of Ibiza swell.

SCENE ONE

Four years earlier. Ibiza club noises emanate from a laptop which NICOLA stares at. We hear the noise of the club. The music. We hear the groans and the cheers from the crowd.

NICOLA: Fuck.

Pause.

Fuck fuck fuck fuck fuck fuck.

She screams. NICOLA starts to hit herself. A couple of times at first.

But then it builds to a frenzy. She climbs into bed. She climbs under the covers and hides. She mutters to herself.

SCENE TWO

That evening. Nicola's bedroom. GINA and NICOLA are watching a screen. GINA is horrified.

GINA: Holy fuck, Nicola.

NICOLA: Please just watch it.

GINA: How long is this?

NICOLA: Seven minutes.

GINA: Christ, Nicola.

NICOLA: I'm turning it off.

GINA: No.

Pause.

Does Adam know?

NICOLA: Obviously not.

GINA: Jesus, Nicola, this'll kill him.

NICOLA: Don't tell him.

Pause.

GINA: When did this happen?

NICOLA: At Boomerang. It was the end of season party.

GINA: Oh, coz' that's fine then?

NICOLA: That's not helpful.

GINA: Are there more videos?

NICOLA: No.

GINA: *(Beat.)* Okay. How long is he saying you've got?

NICOLA: A week and then he'll post it.

GINA: Okay. *(Beat.)* Okay. Okay. Don't panic.

NICOLA: No, you're panicking, Gina. Which is unhelpful, so stop.

The video ends abruptly. They clock it. GINA gets up and puts her shoes on.

(Beat.) What are you doing?

GINA: Well, obviously we're going to the police.

NICOLA: No. Fuck off. No.

GINA: Nicola, the police will help. I understand how scary this is, okay. I understand that this is horrible. I understand that this hasn't happened to me so it's easy for me to say. But you need help. *(Beat.)* Mum needs to know too.

NICOLA: Oh hilarious.

GINA: This isn't a joke, Nicola. Christ, what will everyone say at freshers?

NICOLA: They'll probably call me a slut and a whore.

Pause.

Gina, I'm going to post it on Facebook.

GINA: Nicola, are you mad? The police will sort it.

NICOLA: They can't help me, okay. And I sure as fuck can't find ten thousand euros so I've got to. What choice do I have?

GINA: Don't be so stupid, Nicola. That's stupid. You're not thinking. You've got all the choice.

NICOLA: No I don't, because he's going to upload that video. If I upload it then it's mine.

GINA: You'd be ruined. You'd be 'that' girl.

NICOLA: So I wait for him to start blackmailing me every month? I have to, Gina.

GINA: Give me time. I will make this go away.

NICOLA: Gina, this isn't the *Sopranos.*

GINA: This is our family, Nicola. It's not just you. This will destroy Mum. You're so stupid. What the fuck were you thinking?

NICOLA: Go on, say it.

GINA: You're disgusting. *(Beat.)* I love you.

Please don't do anything else stupid. Give me that laptop.

NICOLA: No.

CHLOE comes bouncing in.

CHLOE: You're hooooooooome.

NICOLA: Chlo.

CHLOE: What's wrong?

GINA: Nothing's wrong.

CHLOE: I'm talking to Nicola.

NICOLA: I'm fine.

CHLOE: Lies. Both of you. You're both being weird. Dinner's ready.

NICOLA: I'm not hungry.

CHLOE: Mum made you burritos, you ungrateful whore.

GINA: Chloe.

CHLOE: It's a nice thing. Like bad bitch. Adam's downstairs.

NICOLA: What?

CHLOE: It was meant to be a surprise, but I know how much you hate surprises so I figured I'd warn you so you could put some nice underwear on. Shave your legs. You can thank me later.

GINA: Adam's downstairs?

CHLOE: Yeah, he's passed his accounting exams. That was meant to be a surprise too. He brought prosecco, but –

NICOLA: Adam?

CHLOE: Yeah.

NICOLA: Downstairs?

CHLOE: No, Ru Paul in the attic. Yes, Adam downstairs, what's so fucking-?

GINA: *(To NICOLA.)* Shall we put the laptop down and have dinner?

NICOLA: No.

GINA: We can talk after.

CHLOE: Talk about what?

GINA: Nicola. I think it would be best. For the whole family. If you came downstairs.

CHLOE: Talk about what?

GINA: *(To CHLOE.)* How was school today?

CHLOE: I know what you're doing.

GINA: Well in that case start behaving like a grown up and give us some fucking space.

CHLOE: Ooh it must be bad. Can I tell Adam?

NICOLA: Tell Adam what?

CHLOE: Whatever you've done. Can I tell him?

NICOLA: There's nothing. I'm coming down now. Please? I just need a minute, okay, Gina? *(Beat.)* Okay, Gina?

Pause.

GINA: Okay.

NICOLA: …

GINA and CHLOE leave. NICOLA is left alone.

NICOLA approaches the laptop. She types for a while. She takes a deep breath. And then … She clicks and it's done. We hear the whoosh of the video uploading.

ADAM enters with a bottle of prosecco.

ADAM: Hi.

NICOLA: Hi.

Pause.

ADAM: So. I've been doing a sudoku with your mum for half an hour.

(Beat.) Chloe said you were coming down.

NICOLA: I am.

ADAM: I've been trying to get hold of you for days.

NICOLA's phone rings. Throughout the rest of the scene social media alerts on NICOLA's phone can ping intermittently or where desired.

Do you want to get that?

NICOLA: No, leave it.

ADAM: Have I done something wrong?

NICOLA: No, not at all. You haven't done anything.

ADAM: Nicola, what's going on?

NICOLA: I love you. So much.

ADAM: Look at me. Tell me what's going on.

NICOLA: Can we have sex?

ADAM: … Nicola, you're scaring me.

NICOLA: Sorry.

ADAM: That's okay. I'm sorry if it wasn't a nice surprise.

NICOLA: This was a lovely surprise.

ADAM: Come here.

ADAM crosses over to her. He tentatively holds out his arms. NICOLA reluctantly crawls into them. Nicola's phone rings.

Do you need to get that?

NICOLA: Leave it. Please.

ADAM kisses her.

Hi.

NICOLA: Hi.

ADAM: What's going on?

NICOLA: Kiss me again.

ADAM: Talk to me.

NICOLA: Kiss me.

ADAM kisses her.

ADAM: What's going on?

NICOLA: I want you. Now. Fuck me.

ADAM: Nicola, you're upset.

NICOLA: I think … I think this is gonna be the last time you're gonna want to have sex with me.

ADAM: That's insane. I'll always think you're amazing.

NICOLA: You don't know.

ADAM: What's happened? *(Beat.)* Has something bad happened?

NICOLA's phone goes off again.

Who is that?

NICOLA: It doesn't matter.

ADAM: Nicola, have you cheated on me?

NICOLA: No.

ADAM: Then I don't understand you.

NICOLA grabs ADAM and kisses him.

ADAM is blindsided.

NICOLA: I want you. Hold me. Just – be with me. Now. I need you.

Please. Look at me.

The phone rings again. They start to remove their clothes. We hear the mounting noise of the phone mixed with message alerts, cameras snapping, a gathering crowd and then the noise of the video until we are deafened.

COMMENTS A

Comments.

TROLL: FUCK ME SHE BE SKANKY.

TROLL: her pussy must be so sore

TROLL: I'm posting out of sheer frustration at how this has been allowed to happen.

TROLL: Lol me wanna fuk dat

TROLL: This is really upsetting

TROLL: RT This is really upsetting someones frigid

TROLL: OH MY GOD I THINK I KNOW HER

TROLL: Wen did this happen

TROLL: The incident took place last week at the nightclub Boomerang in Ibiza at their end of season fiesta.

TROLL: Is anyone reporting it?

TROLL: Don't think the police are involved think she loved it

TROLL: These men have taken this young lady's reputation!!! This is a scandal and a disgrace!!! No lady could want this!!! Hilary.

TROLL: YOUNG GIRL PERFORMING EXPLICIT SEX ACT IN IBIZA CLICK LINK BELOW FOR FULL VID YUM YUM

TROLL: ONE NIPPLE DARKER THAN THE OTHER THO

TROLL: That wat jizz is for

TROLL: YOUNG GIRL IN IBIZA SEX VIDEO NAMED AS NICOLA BARKER CLICK LINK BELOW FOR FULL VID YUM YUM

TROLL: BORED PANDA QUIZ which dick in the ibiza video are you?

TROLL: Fuck me I do know her I used to sit next to her in maths nice legs

TROLL: Id shove a knife between her nice legs lol

TROLL: RT IF YOU'RE POSTING FROM SPAIN

TROLL: you can see someone's hit her cervix at 0.59, her eyes roll back.

TROLL: RT you can see someone's hit her cervix at 0.59, her eyes roll back. THIS IS DANGEROUS. THESE ARE HER REPRODUCTIVE ORGANS.

TROLL: I have never slept with anyone is this what group sex is it looks frightening we don't have this in denmark

TROLL: LOL DENMARK

TROLL: WHERE NICOLA BARKER LIVE WOOF?

TROLL: I mean … Every day a girl turns 18, right?

SCENE THREE

The next morning. NICOLA and CHLOE are sat on NICOLA's bed. We can hear distant hubub.

CHLOE: I reckon we could negotiate that one up though? Or there's this.

GINA enters.

GINA: What the fuck have you done?

NICOLA: Gina, calm down.

CHLOE: Yeah, Gina, calm down.

GINA: Have you looked outside?

CHLOE: They started turning up just after you left for work. I've had the day off school. It's brilliant.

GINA: Christ. You were meant to give me time.

NICOLA: I had no idea this was going to happen when I posted it, okay? I didn't know.

GINA: It's on Buzzfeed.

NICOLA: Is it really?

CHLOE: Cool.

NICOLA: That's mad.

GINA: You're in shock.

NICOLA: No, I'm not.

GINA: You don't understand what you've done.

NICOLA: I do. I didn't want to spend the rest of my life with this hanging over my head.

CHLOE: Better out than in.

NICOLA: I'm relieved, Geen.

GINA: You've just sabotaged your life. You've ruined our lives.

CHLOE: What are you talking about? This is amazing. I'm going to make her money.

GINA: What?

CHLOE: I didn't go to school today.

GINA: Bravo.

CHLOE: And I went outside and took all their business cards and said she'd do an interview for the highest bider.

GINA: You did what?

CHLOE: They're all emailing me.

GINA: Turn your phone off right now.

CHLOE: Kevin from The Daily Mail is nice. I made him a cup of tea.

GINA: Chloe, these are real people. They don't care about Nicola like we do.

CHLOE: You don't care about Nicola. You've just barged in and said she's ruined your life.

GINA: This isn't a game. Nicola's not stupid enough to do an interview and you're not a PA.

NICOLA: Gina.

GINA: What?

NICOLA: I've been thinking.

CHLOE: She's been thinking with me.

NICOLA: Gina, I need people to know my side of the story. I think it's important.

GINA: You're not serious?

NICOLA: You don't know how this feels.

CHLOE: Yeah, you don't know.

GINA: GET OUT, CHLOE.

CHLOE: NO.

GINA: Go downstairs and look after mum.

CHLOE: You do it. She smashed a bottle of red and now she's crying with a tub of Vanish in the living room. I'm not going anywhere. This is my deal. I'm involved now whether you like it or not and –

GINA: Get out. Just get out everyone just – get – I –

GINA starts to cry with anger. NICOLA and CHLOE don't know what to do. CHLOE gets up and leaves.

You don't know what you're doing.

NICOLA: Yes, I do. I want to.

GINA: Adam doesn't deserve this. What did you tell him?

NICOLA: …

GINA: You spoke to him last night?

NICOLA: I couldn't, Gina. His face – I just couldn't.

GINA: That is beyond cruel.

NICOLA: This isn't happening to him, this is happening to me, now, and I need you with me so stop fucking judging me.

GINA: You're nineteen. You don't know what you want.

NICOLA: I want an interview.

GINA: Tell me I'm not hearing this.

NICOLA: That man's not winning my life, Gina.

GINA: They'll twist all your words.

NICOLA: At least I'll get the last word. People want to hear what I have to say.

GINA: And what do you have to say?

NICOLA: I'm not a slut. I'm ordinary. I'm me. I need people to know that.

GINA: Oh 'coz seeking media attention after what you've done really sells that.

NICOLA: If you don't help me then I'll ask Chloe.

GINA: She's a child.

NICOLA: She's not being a child right now.

GINA: You are both being children.

CHLOE enters.

CHLOE: You started talking about me so I figured I'd come back in. Look, my phone is going off the chain here so can we talk about it because The Mail have offered twenty thousand.

Pause.

GINA: Twenty thousand?

NICOLA: Fuck.

CHLOE: I'm as surprised as you. I love you, Nic, but you're not worth twenty thousand.

GINA: You are on seriously thin ice, Chloe.

CHLOE: I'd pretend to be scared, Geen, but I'm too busy trying to secure us a deal. Actually, do you reckon its worth more? Must be if they've gone in at twenty. I might tweet Katie Hopkins. See what she thinks. Vice have offered way less but, you know, edgy. Contact's Alex Campbell. She seems nice. And a woman.

GINA: Sit down.

CHLOE: Look I didn't know that a video of Nic masturbating would be so popular either but this is what's happened so instead of lecturing her and being a bitch about it, how about we help?

Silence.

GINA: A video of what?

CHLOE: *(Beat.)* A video of … Nic masturbating.

GINA: You haven't seen it?

CHLOE: I – Well, like I assumed 'coz … 'coz they're all outside saying Nic's done a sex tape and it's wasn't Adam 'coz they said it was on holiday and Adam wasn't on holiday he stayed here so it wasn't with Adam so I thought …

Pause.

GINA: I'd like her to watch it.

NICOLA: Gina.

CHLOE: Yeah, I want to watch it.

GINA: Go on.

NICOLA: Gina, don't you dare.

GINA: Don't Gina me, if you two are silly enough to sit there and think you've got this under control –

GINA gets the laptop out and finds the video.

Fuck, it's trending.

NICOLA: She's a child.

GINA: She was a child when you let her contact the press for you an hour ago.

CHLOE: Come on then, just fucking show me.

GINA: Alright then.

CHLOE: I want to.

GINA: Well good.

CHLOE: Fine.

> *GINA presses play. NICOLA looks at the wall. GINA watches CHLOE. CHLOE watches the video. She is visibly shocked. She tries not to let her distress show on her face. She becomes fascinated. She hardens.*

GINA: That's enough now.

CHLOE: Wait.

> *CHLOE watches a bit more.*

GINA: I said that's enough.

CHLOE: Okay.

> *CHLOE lowers the lid of the laptop.*
>
> *Silence.*

Vice. *(Beat.)* It's less money, but you should go with Vice.

(Beat.) The Mail would eat you alive for that.

COMMENTS B

Comments.

TROLL: She's fucking shameless

TROLL: Lol at Alex Campbell's questions

TROLL: This is just one big lol

TROLL: I reckon she's done pretty well. Think about all the awful things that could have been said.

TROLL: FUCK OFF GRANDMA

TROLL: I particularly like the flick of the hair when she says she doesn't feel victimised. What a cool collected customer!! ;)

TROLL: I'd victimise her until she begged for more

TROLL: She's so fucking clam.

TROLL: Where is her lipstick from? Anyone pleeeeease?

TROLL: So fucking CALM.

TROLL: I watched to gloat but I have to say she's pretty fucking savvy.

TROLL: She made me laugh

TROLL: RT she made me laugh NO WOMAN HAS EVER MADE ANYONE LAUGH EVER. FACT.

TROLL: GO HOME AND SEE IF YOU'RE DICK'S STILL THERE.

TROLL: I kinda like her

SCENE FOUR

Later that evening. ADAM is in NICOLA's bedroom. He is shaking.

NICOLA: Say something.

> *Pause.*

ADAM: Do you want me to break up with you?

NICOLA: No.

ADAM: Do you have any idea? I mean any idea at all what I've been going through?

NICOLA: No.

ADAM: No, you don't.

> *Silence.*

> I watched it.

> *Silence.*

> Everyone on my course had already seen it. Didn't want to miss out. *(Beat.)* Doesn't even look like you. At all.

NICOLA: I don't know what to say to that.

ADAM: Last night you let me fuck you. You begged me to fuck you.

NICOLA: …

ADAM: How could you do that after … what you did? Did you use condoms?

Silence.

Oh fuck you, Nicola.

NICOLA: I'm sorry.

ADAM: Fuck. You fucking –

NICOLA: I'm sorry. I'm so sorry.

ADAM: I want to know why.

NICOLA: I don't know.

ADAM: Am I not enough for you?

NICOLA: You are.

ADAM: Was I not enough for you last night?

NICOLA: Adam.

ADAM: People have been laughing at me. Everyone's laughing at me. My own father is laughing at me.

NICOLA: I love you.

ADAM: Do you?

NICOLA nods.

Say it.

NICOLA: I just did.

ADAM: Say it again.

NICOLA: I … I love you.

ADAM: No, *I* love *you*. And I have always treated you with respect because that is how people in love treat each other.

NICOLA: I do love you.

ADAM: I wanted to be with you forever. *(Beat.)* Take your clothes off.

NICOLA: Adam.

ADAM: Is that how you want to be treated? Because I can. I can do that. I can call you a whore and make you bend over for me.

Go on. Get down on your knees, you whore.

NICOLA: I want you and I'm sorry.

ADAM: Say it again.

NICOLA: I'm sorry. I'm sorry I'm sorry I'm sorry I'm sorry I'm sorry.

(Beat.) I'm sorry.

ADAM: I never thought I'd want to hit a woman.

NICOLA: So hit me.

ADAM: *(Beat.)* No.

NICOLA: If it'd make you feel better.

ADAM: No, it'd make *you* feel better. So I won't. *(Beat.)* You did things with those men that we've never even talked about.

NICOLA: …

ADAM: We could have done those things.

NICOLA: Do you want to do those things?

ADAM: … I don't know. Maybe I do. Maybe I did. I'll never know now.

I'd always thought that good people wouldn't want to do those things. *(Beat.)* I don't know what I want.

NICOLA: I love you.

ADAM: Stop talking. Just shut up. Shut the fuck up.

Pause.

I'm going to the walk-in clinic now to see what you've given me.

NICOLA: No.

ADAM: Get Gina to bring me anything of mine. Or burn it. I don't want it. I don't want you.

NICOLA: Don't. Don't leave me.

ADAM: If there hadn't been a video … would you have even told me?

Pause.

You're disgusting. *(Beat.)* Fuck you.

NICOLA: You don't get to leave. None of my friends are talking to me. Mum's not talking to me. Gina's talking to me but thinks I'm a whore. But you don't. You can't leave. Because, if you leave, Adam, then I'll have nothing left. And I mean nothing. *(Beat.)* And there'll be nothing to stop me doing anything.

COMMENTS C

Comments.

TROLL: Fap fap fap fap fap

TROLL: LMAO

TROLL: Please keep the thread clean, thank you Hilary :)

TROLL: OMG the way she shakes Alex Campbell's hand it's like I'll have what she's having k thanx byeeeee #nicforpresident

TROLL: Where can I tap that?

TROLL: She's single lads let's go round her house and give her some sex

TROLL: her top is sold out at h&m so annoying me likey :)

TROLL: is she really single?

TROLL: it's not rape if you shout surprise it's a present

TROLL: She's fucking fabulous

SCENE FIVE

A day later. NICOLA's in bed. GINA enters with two cups of tea.

GINA: How are you feeling?

NICOLA: Kind of wonderful.

GINA: I meant about Adam.

NICOLA: I've been thinking about what Alex Campbell said. It was good advice, because my next move would be crucial. I couldn't be half in half out about it. The next move I make would have to be like, 'this is me'. 'This is what I'm about'.

GINA: You don't have to make a move.

NICOLA: The only thing is there are people out there now who know me for 'that'.

GINA: Right.

NICOLA: And those people really like 'that'.

GINA: You don't actually wanna do 'that' again, do you?

NICOLA: On holiday I felt free to … be like that.

GINA: How come?

NICOLA: I felt … removed. In a good way. There but not. And because I felt *that* it felt good and not bad.

GINA: Did it feel good?

NICOLA: Like my scalp and the soles of my feet were on fire.

GINA: I don't know what that means.

Pause.

NICOLA: I could do a webcam.

GINA: *(Beat.)* A webcam?

NICOLA: I think it could be quite cute.

GINA: What's cute?

NICOLA: Okay. So, I'd be a good girl who went on holiday and fell from grace who's back in the UK and curious. I'd take specific requests from my channel subscribers.

GINA: Nicola, that's huge.

NICOLA: I don't have to do it. I'd just have to engage.

GINA: What's the difference?

NICOLA: Well, like, I'll have to do some things, yeah. Obviously. But not every little thing they demand. This would be be classy. High production quality. We'd set the bar high. I'm new to the industry. I'm virginal as far as the industry is concerned.

GINA: Oh right and where is your high production quality coming from?

NICOLA: You can sit here and try and talk me down all you want Gina, but I'm sure about this. I'm surer than I've ever been. Today was … Look, that interview I gave today was totally disarming. It was beguiling and seductive and powerful. I know it was because I saw their faces. I saw yours too. That and it's trending on twitter. *(Beat.)* I can't do this without you.

GINA: Is that right?

NICOLA: I don't want to do this without you.

GINA: Then don't do it at all.

NICOLA: Gina, I'm doing this. I want to.

GINA: I don't understand.

NICOLA: You don't have to. You just have to be there.

GINA: What?

NICOLA: Because you're my manager now.

GINA: What? Why?

NICOLA: Why not? No one's ever gonna protect me like you, so you might as well. Listen, I enjoyed today. I had a fucking ball.

GINA: Yeah, you had a ball *today*. You'd be gambling away your whole life off the back of one good interview. You can't come back from this. Once you go in–

NICOLA: Don't fight me. There's no point. *(Beat.)* I think you want this. I think you'd be good at this. I think this excites you.

GINA: No, it doesn't.

NICOLA: It does, Geen, because you're scared. And all scary things are exciting.

GINA: Leave my job to help you lie on your back?

NICOLA: Then get out. Go on then. Fuck off. I want people on my team. If you're not on my team then fuck off. I don't need a mother, I've already got one.

GINA: Grow up.

NICOLA: I have. I want this and you want this.

GINA: All I want is for you to be okay.

NICOLA: I'm better than I've ever been. Look, if it's trolling you're worried about, surviving it's a piece of piss. Anyone can do it. You have to be totally transparent. Simple as. We can have personal feelings, but we can't have secrets. Any shit that hits the fan, we make money from it and claim back the ownership. It can't fail. *(Beat.)* He took something from me. And I got it back. This way I can't lose.

GINA: Define winning.

CHLOE enters without knocking.

Knock, Chlo.

CHLOE: It's not your room.

NICOLA: How was school?

CHLOE: You look like an Instagram.

NICOLA: Thanks.

CHLOE: Why aren't you at work, Gina?

NICOLA: I wanted her home with me.

CHLOE: You two have done nothing but sit up here and whisper since I set up that interview and I've had to sit downstairs and talk to Mum with her red wine smile.

GINA: Chloe.

CHLOE: What was she like?

GINA: Who?

CHLOE: Alex Campbell at Vice. Was she nice?

GINA: Stop it, Chloe.

CHLOE: No, I'm not going to stop it because it isn't fair. And yes, before you accuse me of being a teenager, I am a teenager. Deal with it. And you know what? Teenagers often say 'it's not fair' because we're not frightened of saying the truth. And I'm saying the truth now. It's not fair. I'm your sister too and you've done nothing but huddle.

GINA: Nic needs a big sister right now, Chlo. The same way you might one day.

CHLOE: Well, that's retarded because what you're saying is no one will ever need little sisters and they're just there to amuse or something and I love you just as much as Geen loves you. You can't measure love because you were born first.

GINA: I'm not saying that.

CHLOE: I'm sick of being left out.

GINA: We're not leaving you out of anything.

CHLOE: Where's my cut of the money I made you?

GINA: What money?

CHLOE: Oh whatever. Go on then. Go and fuck it all up. Don't come crying to me, Gina, when I've got a nice house and children and all you'll have is twenty cats and a cobweb vagina and Nicola's doing blow jobs for coke in the city centre round the back of Burger King.

GINA: How was school?

CHLOE: School was shit. Ms Regan did an announcement in front of the whole class about what Nicola had done and how everyone had to be nice to me and it was pizza for lunch and I couldn't have any because I'm on a diet and I finally got my period and bled all over a reading room chair.

Pause.

GINA: Chloe.

CHLOE: I just want a tampon.

She stretches out her hand.

NICOLA: Do you know how to-?

CHLOE: Don't fucking patronise me.

Beat. NICOLA gets up and gives CHLOE a box of tampons. CHLOE takes the box and exits. We see her on the landing. She debates going back in. She stands on the landing reading the leaflet on how to insert the tampon. She keeps looking back at the door.

GINA: Have you spoken to Mum?

NICOLA: Obviously not.

GINA: You'll break her heart, Nic.

NICOLA: I won't. I'm still me. Feelings can be sorted out later. We need to nail this next move and make sure it goes well. That way she won't mind because we'll have smashed it.

GINA: We?

NICOLA: I'm offering double what you make at reception. *(Beat.)* Webcamming. Come on, Geen. Are you with me?

GINA: …

NICOLA has won.

SCENE SIX

A day later. ADAM is pacing around NICOLA's bedroom.

ADAM: I don't understand. You want me to be in them with you?

NICOLA: No. No.

ADAM: But you want to do this with other people?

NICOLA: No. God no, just me. It's just me.

ADAM: But people are gonna see you naked.

NICOLA: Online, yes.

ADAM: I don't know why I came.

NICOLA: I'm happy you did.

ADAM: … But I'm a really nice person, Nicola. I'm really fucking nice.

NICOLA: No one's saying you're not.

ADAM: I can't sleep. I want to hate you but I can't. I just can't fucking – God, I'm angry. You make me fucking angry.

NICOLA: I'm sorry.

ADAM: Do not say you're sorry. *(Beat.)* Have you always wanted to do this?

NICOLA: No. I – No.

ADAM: But now you do? *(Beat.)* I need to hear it, Nic.

NICOLA: Okay. I'm feeling curious. And that curiosity is overwhelming. Like I'm scared. But good scared. I just need to jump. Or run. Just fucking … go. That's how I feel.

I know how much I've hurt you. But you're my only sturdy thing.

ADAM: Cheers. I'll be here in the corner shall I? Dependable old Adam. Like a toothless labrador.

NICOLA: That's not what I meant. I need you, Adam, I can't do this without you.

ADAM: *(Beat.)* Anything else happen that I should know about? That wasn't on the video.

NICOLA: No.

ADAM: You swear?

NICOLA: You're going to have to trust me.

ADAM laughs.

ADAM: What do you want?

NICOLA: I want you.

ADAM: So you keep saying.

NICOLA: What do you want?

ADAM punches a pillow. He punches it until it is 'dead'. He kisses NICOLA roughly. They start to take off their clothes. He stops. He looks at her body. He goes to his bag and pulls out a condom. He goes back over to NICOLA and carries on.

COMMENTS D

Comments.

TROLL: She's uglier than the chicks I usually rape ;)

SCENE SEVEN

Two days later. GINA waits on the landing. She checks her watch. CHLOE enters. They watch each other.

GINA: She's – um … She's having a moment.

CHLOE: What a surprise.

GINA: Not now, Chloe.

CHLOE sighs and hands GINA a can of hairspray and a hairbrush with a long handle.

What's this?

CHLOE: These are for the video you're making.

Pause.

GINA: What video?

CHLOE: 'What video?'

NICOLA moans from the other side of the door. Pause.

GINA: Thanks, Chlo. She's done her hair already.

CHLOE: They're not for her hair.

Pause.

I reckon if you have full on toys it might be a bit scary, or whatever. These might be crap. It's just a suggestion. I figured since it's the first one you're doing. Like a home-made one. I dunno … I just thought they were … relatable.

Pause.

I can help.

Pause.

GINA: Chloe, you're a child and this is grown up stuff.

CHLOE: You're making porn. And I want to help. Gina, I know what sex is. I've seen porn. I masturbate. I don't get what the big deal is. We're all adults now. It's a society thing. I am an adult because life already has adult expectations of me. So there.

GINA: This isn't a game, Chloe. You wouldn't know the first thing.

CHLOE: Please. What experience do you have? You man the phones at Foxtons. How are you going to do this? *(Beat.)* Are you quitting your job?

GINA: It's important she's supervised.

CHLOE: The fuck? Who the fuck do you think you are? If you can work for Nicola then I can work for Nicola. Do you even want this? Because I'd love this. And if you don't want this then you should probably say.

NICOLA moans.

GINA: If Nicola wants this. Then yes.

Pause.

CHLOE: Okay. Then I get to help.

GINA: *(Beat.)* What could you help with?

CHLOE: I want social media. Branding's really important. I saw it on *The Apprentice.* Plus it's my dream job.

GINA: What is?

CHLOE: I want to be a ghost tweeter.

GINA: That's not a thing.

CHLOE: Then I feel sorry for you and this is going to fail because you're a lot naïver than I thought because if we can get her trending again we might be in a position to crowdsource user-generated content which strengthens brands and I'm not sure you even know what that means. *(Beat.)* She's my sister too. I'm not leaving. And if you don't let me in I'll tell mum.

Silence.

GINA: Don't tell Mum.

CHLOE pushes past GINA and barges in.

COMMENTS E

Comments.

TROLL: Her cunt must reek.

TROLL: These comments are truly saddening. This blog is meant to help. That is all. Tim, 49, Wiltshire.

TROLL: Holy fuck I've never seen ne1 take hairbrush that deep

TROLL: so cute she is so bashful with the hairbrush like she has naughty secret to share from her room very attractive ;)

TROLL: Oh I'm sorry little Instagram white girl that we fucked up your day by telling the truth you fucking whore I will cut a hole in your cheek and rape it until I'm done. Fuk you.

SCENE EIGHT

Six months later. NICOLA has just walked in. ADAM is sitting on the end of the bed with a laptop.

NICOLA: Oh my god.

ADAM: It's not what it looks like.

NICOLA: Okay.

ADAM: It isn't. I wasn't wanking. I – God, Nicola, you can't just walk in.

NICOLA: It's my room.

NICOLA sits down next to him. He can't look at her.

Fuck, Adam. We agreed you wouldn't watch them.

ADAM: I'm so fucking embarrassed.

NICOLA: *You're* embarrassed?

ADAM: Don't say that.

NICOLA: Why didn't you tell me?

ADAM: How the fuck could I?

NICOLA: We agreed you wouldn't watch them.

ADAM: If it were that simple, Nic, then I wouldn't watch them. But it's not.

NICOLA: Hang on, how have you been watching them? Have you been paying for them?

Pause.

Adam, the videos are really expensive.

ADAM: I don't give a fuck. It's not about the money. I just … They're out there. And when I sit on the tube every time I look up I sit there looking at the men. And I think, which of you's seen her. Who's watching her. Who's seen her naked.

NICOLA: I don't think that.

ADAM: I keep picturing them cumming watching you and it's like … It's like they're fucking you and I don't know. Like they're raping you but I don't know and you're smiling and laughing while they're sliding out of you and you're covered in their cum and I don't know. And I can't bear it. You're walking around and their cum's all over you and I don't know. Why do you pretend you're single?

NICOLA: *(Beat.)* Adam. Because – because it makes the brand stronger. Because more people watch them then, because money, Adam.

ADAM: I can give you money.

NICOLA: I don't care about that.

ADAM: If you don't care about it then tell them you've got a boyfriend.

NICOLA: You know I can't do that. *(Beat.)* I love you.

ADAM: Like you love camming?

NICOLA: Don't.

ADAM: When was the last time we slept together?

NICOLA: That's not fair.

ADAM: See? You never want to.

NICOLA: I'm tired.

ADAM: Be tired with me then. Let's have tired lazy sex, that'd be nice. I'd bloody love that.

NICOLA: I need a shower.

ADAM: I could join you?

NICOLA: No, on my own.

ADAM: You have a lot of fun on your own.

NICOLA: Meaning?

ADAM: You look so happy.

NICOLA: They're not real. They're like fucking … Facebook. You know? They're not real.

ADAM: They are real, Nicola, because you're doing it.

NICOLA: The feelings aren't real. What I look like I'm feeling isn't real.

ADAM: Then why am I feeling everything?

SCENE NINE

A year later. NICOLA's bedroom. NICOLA is signing pictures of herself. GINA is on a headset taking a call. CHLOE enters and sits down with her school bag. She gets her books out and takes the laptop from GINA while she's on the phone. It's a familiar action.

GINA: What's that?

Yes, of course, only I've just had a look over the contract and the wording here's rather vague.

Sure. Sure, I hear what you're saying. I totally do, it's just we'd want to talk minutiae about what's being –

Right. If you're telling me, please do correct me if I've got this wrong, but if you're telling me that's the sole area your readership are interested in, what with you being a niche publication, with, albeit a very wide, uh, readership, then that's what's being referred to in the wording?

Ah, I would, only our schedule's rammed and we're trying to –

Ha, yes. Nightmare.

Thank you.

She wildly gestures at CHLOE. CHLOE starts typing like a demon. She runs over with the laptop and shows GINA the screen.

Well it's been lovely talking to you, *James.*

GINA gives CHLOE the thumbs up as she sits back down.

Thank you, James. We'll ring you by tomorrow to confirm.

Okay?

Yep, you too. Bye.

GINA takes the headset off and gives it to CHLOE.

Well, you're not doing that.

NICOLA: Oh?

GINA: They're into pee. Why were we even talking to them? Who contacted them?

CHLOE: I did. It's a lot of money they're offering, Geen. Nic can always say no.

CHLOE takes a water bottle out of her bag and pours it into a glass by the side of NICOLA's bed. It's a green liquid.

CHLOE arranges the glass and puts a colourful straw in it from her bag. She snaps a photo with her phone.

I heart green juice. Hashtag healthy hashtag thursday hashtag love yourself hashtag inside and out hashtag libido hashtag healthy is hot.

She shows it to NICOLA and GINA.

GINA: Not clickbaity enough.

CHLOE: Okay. Got it. 'You'll never guess what's in this? Hashtag my secret weapon hashtag comment for clues hashtag healthy hashtag thursday hashtag love yourself hashtag inside and out hashtag libido hashtag healthy is hot.'

GINA: Perfect. Tweet it.

CHLOE: No, wait. I'm adding hashtag waistline. Boom.

NICOLA goes to take a sip.

Oh don't, Nic, it's paint. Oh, fuck. *(Beat.)* I forgot.

NICOLA: What?

CHLOE: I took an offer from Lovebox. They rang this morning and couriered over a crate of toys. They've said we get to proof the final edit before it goes out tomorrow, but it's an exclusive with Nicola Barker road testing their new products. It's for their private channels. They've said if they can just get a shot of you enjoying each toy? Oh, except … There was one. Oh yep, the butt plug. They're all in the same price range pretty much, apart from the butt plug which is weighted and vibrates so they're keen to flog that one.

GINA: When did you take this?

CHLOE: A week ago.

GINA: A week ago?

CHLOE: I'm sorry, I've been rushed off my feet. I forgot.

GINA: *How* did you take this?

CHLOE: At school. *(Beat.)* I might have said I was you.

GINA: Chloe.

CHLOE: Sorry.

NICOLA: Where are the toys?

CHLOE: They couriered them.

GINA: To school?

CHLOE: I had them delivered to modern languages. No-one goes there.

GINA: Bloody hell.

CHLOE: I'm sorry. I forgot to mention it. It's only going to take half an hour. I worked it out. Three toys and finish with the butt plug.

NICOLA: I had the rest of that left over curry for lunch.

CHLOE: Oh.

NICOLA: For fuck's sake. And you're saying they need this by tomorrow?

CHLOE: By tonight. I'm so sorry, Nic. I totally forgot. I had coursework –

NICOLA: I don't feel comfortable using a plug knowing –

GINA: Shit.

NICOLA: It's okay. Right. This is what we're going to do –

GINA: Well, we're calling Lovebox and cancelling.

CHLOE: Um, Geen … We've been playing kiss chase with Lovebox for two weeks. I'm not losing this because Nic's got no self control.

NICOLA: Self control? I was eating lunch.

GINA: We're cancelling.

CHLOE: I took an advance.

GINA: // What?

NICOLA: // Sorry?

CHLOE: It'll be in the company account. They transferred half up front. I signed it off.

GINA: Jesus Christ, Chloe.

NICOLA: Make yourself useful.

CHLOE: Like how?

NICOLA: Go and run me a shallow bath and make sure Mum
doesn't come in. Luke warm.

CHLOE leaves the room.

GINA: What's your plan?

NICOLA: A makeshift bidet it is.

GINA: You can't give yourself an enema.

NICOLA: I've done it before.

GINA: Chloe's a little shit. This is all a bit …

NICOLA: What?

GINA: You're tired.

NICOLA: I'm working.

GINA: You're knackered.

NICOLA: I'm not.

GINA: You look awful.

NICOLA: Cheers.

GINA: Nicola, do you want to do this forever?

Pause.

NICOLA: …

GINA: Did you know that we've made a hundred and seventy k?

CHLOE re-enters with the toys.

CHLOE: Bath's running. I got you a nice new razor head.
Be careful. Geen and I will test the batteries and get the
towels and wipes and stuff.

NICOLA: Thanks.

CHLOE: Is there anything you'd like?

NICOLA: Um … Could I have some water?

CHLOE: Sure. And for after?

NICOLA: A cup of tea?

CHLOE: Yup.

GINA: I'm sorry, but I'm not going to sit here and pretend that everything's okay. She's got dark circles under her eyes. We are gambling with her reproductive health.

CHLOE: You sound like a sex ed VHS.

NICOLA: Look, I am a bit tired, but I'm fine. Everyone gets tired at work. I love my job.

GINA: You can't do this forever, Nicola. We could get out now. You could buy somewhere for you and Adam to live.

CHLOE: She's just getting started. If this is what she can make in a year then what can she make in two? Three? Supply and demand, Gina.

GINA: Yes, but we cannot keep up with the demand because the supply is our sister.

CHLOE: I know, I'm just saying that the very fact that demand is high is one fucking solid reason for her to stay in the business.

GINA: This isn't your decision.

CHLOE: Well it is actually, because all three of us have a stake in this.

NICOLA: Actually it's mine.

CHLOE: Right.

NICOLA: And I don't want to stop now.

CHLOE: Thank you.

GINA: Why, though? Why don't you want to stop?

NICOLA: Because … It's ours, because … Look, if there were a hundred more 'me's then yeah, sure I'd consider stepping back, but there aren't, so I'm not going to. And neither are you. Can you just test the fucking batteries please. I'll be in the bathroom.

NICOLA exits.

GINA: She's exhausted and you're not helping.

CHLOE: You know what's not helping? Reminding her how exhausted she is right before she cams. Now stay and help me or go and have a glass of red with mum. Your call. *(Beat.)* Chill the fuck out. Have a wank. It won't kill you.

GINA exits. CHLOE is left looking at the toys.

COMMENTS F

Comments.

TROLL: LOVED this thanks Nic :)

TROLL: never felt comfortable using a plug before will defs pick one up

TROLL: u look so hot when u cum I wanna take your nipple in my mouth

TROLL: I could take you out to dinner treat u real nice

TROLL: Yum Ive got that plug in now no more haribo for me lol #anal #eatcleanfuckclean

TROLL: A huge thank you from all of us here at Lovebox to naughty Nicola for road testing our new range. Come and get 'em while they're hot ladies! Xx

TROLL: I want to take that plug and use it on you until there's absolutely no way you could ever have children

SCENE TEN

A few days later. The three sisters are watching a laptop. NICOLA and GINA are horrified.

CHLOE: So?

NICOLA: What the fuck?

CHLOE: I haven't uploaded it. I just thought I'd make it and then you guys could approve it. *(Beat.)* I think it's quite good.

GINA: Delete it.

CHLOE: Hey. Why?

GINA: I feel sick. You look at me right now, Chloe Barker, and don't you dare lie to me. Have you uploaded this anywhere?

NICOLA: Have you got this on any other device?

CHLOE: No. I just – It's just on my laptop. I made it to show you guys.

GINA: Delete it now.

NICOLA: Fucking delete it, Chloe.

CHLOE: Okay. *(Beat.)* Right, it's deleted.

GINA: Are you sure? Empty the trash can. Lower right corner.

CHLOE: I've already emptied the bloody trash can, I know how to use a computer. I'm not fifty. There. It's done.

NICOLA: *(Beat.)* What the fuck were you thinking?

CHLOE: I was helping.

NICOLA: How the fuck was that helping?

CHLOE: I'm helping the business.

GINA: You're helping no one.

CHLOE: You know I read the emails, right?

GINA: …

NICOLA: What emails?

CHLOE: I see the stuff we get through. *(Beat.)* We could have made double – triple what we've made in a year.

GINA: You're a child, Chloe.

CHLOE: I'd have done it. If you didn't want to. I don't feel squeamish about making out with Nic. Just holding a vibrator to her. No big deal.

NICOLA: Gina?

GINA: They were inappropriate requests.

NICOLA: But you didn't think to tell me?

CHLOE: Some of them weren't inappropriate. Some of them wanted to see me.

GINA: That is the very definition of inappropriate.

CHLOE: Just 'coz the thought of having an orgasm makes you wanna vom doesn't mean I feel that way. Look, we can't get those bookings back. You haven't protected anybody by pretending those requests didn't come in. You keep saying how tired Nic is.

NICOLA: Gina?

CHLOE: Sorry, Nic, you are tired and you're losing weight in a gross way not a hot way. *I'm* not tired.

NICOLA: Excuse me?

CHLOE: You said 'if there were more of you'.

NICOLA: Yeah, more of *me* not more of *you.*

GINA: This is absolutely ridiculous. I refuse to have a conversation about letting you cam.

CHLOE: But there's a market.

GINA: How do I get this through your thick skull? What you made was child porn.

CHLOE: I'm not a child.

GINA: Yes, you are. In the eyes of the law you're a child. That was child pornography. You made child pornography. We were in possession of child – You would have been taken into care. We would have been arrested.

CHLOE: I'm trying to be proactive here. I'm just trying to save the business.

NICOLA: It doesn't need saving.

CHLOE: It does, Nic, because you're up against your sell-by date. We're not getting the web count or the revenue that we used to and I reckon it might have something to do with the fact that I've seen you yawn in a video.

NICOLA: The fuck?

CHLOE: I can help. Look, our demand is greater than our supply.

GINA: Obviously.

CHLOE: *(To NICOLA.)* Then there needs to be more of you. And if you won't employ me then we need to employ other people. Then, if you're tired, we can showcase more young talent and slowly phase you out.

NICOLA: No one's phasing me out.

GINA: What are you asking, Chloe? You want me to run a brothel?

CHLOE: You wouldn't be running a brothel. It's basically the same thing you're doing now.

NICOLA: You are not currently running a brothel.

GINA: No, I –

NICOLA: Um, Gina, I just want it known at this point that I'm not a prostitute.

GINA: Oh God, of course you're –

NICOLA: I work in sex. I am not a sex worker.

GINA: I know that.

NICOLA: Then why are we talking about brothels?

GINA: I didn't mean –

NICOLA: Good, because I don't sleep with other people for money.

CHLOE: She doesn't sleep with other people for money, Gina.

GINA: I am aware.

CHLOE: Nicola's not a prostitute and you wouldn't be running a brothel.

NICOLA: But on a practical level –

CHLOE: Sex tapes.

GINA: A sex tape business.

CHLOE: That's what we're doing now with a clientele of one. I don't see how it's different.

GINA: It's hugely different.

CHLOE: How?

GINA: Because Nicola's our sister.

CHLOE: We're family, I get that, but that's all a bit mafia. I reckon we can afford to branch out. With Nic at the helm.

NICOLA: How?

CHLOE: You're still the face of the brand. Still totally crucial to the business, still making videos if that's what you want? I'm just saying that we could be dominating the market.

GINA: We are.

CHLOE: I mean the mass market. Consumer generated stuff. I'm just saying we need to think about why this was successful in the first place.

NICOLA: Go on.

CHLOE: I reckon your appeal is that you look piss ordinary.

NICOLA: Cheers.

CHLOE: It's true though. You're not ugly and you're not a Kardashian. You look like a normal person. A normal person that makes porn. People went nuts because it was a real life girls gone wild. Imagine opening this up to other people.

GINA: Okay, but it's porn.

CHLOE: What are we making now? *(Beat.)* What about couples?

NICOLA: Couples?

CHLOE: If they want videos but made in a safe way that's fun. Pitch it high end. I dunno. Just a thought. We could make it like a pop up studio. We could make a few.

GINA: How long have you been planning this, Chloe?

NICOLA: *(To GINA.)* How much did you say we'd made?

GINA: Over my cold dead body, Nicola.

CHLOE: Walk away then. Go back to work. Try and get your old job back after what you've been doing. I dare you. I just won't go back to school. I'll help you Nicola.

NICOLA: We need to think about this properly. A studio then. Good lighting, clean, comfortable. A safe space for girls and boys to have a fucking good time.

CHLOE: Only we can't do it, 'coz Gina wants out.

GINA: I don't want out. I just think we should all slow down.

CHLOE: It's cool, you want out and I want in. No judgement.

NICOLA: Isn't this what you wanted, Gina? For me to stop camming?

GINA: I've never said that.

NICOLA: I like this.

NICOLA gets up.

GINA: Where are you going?

NICOLA: I'm calling Nationwide. Oh and Gina? I want full access to the email accounts from now on please.

GINA: For fuck's sake.

CHLOE: Now everyone can be a Nicola.

COMMENTS G

Comments.

TROLL: Lol so cryptic

TROLL: What do you think it means?

TROLL: I reckon it's like a sex shop you know?

TROLL: Nope I reckon its like a place for people to fuck

TROLL: That would be mental

TROLL: they're announcing on 30th via live cam

TROLL: TEXT 5003 TO DONATE £2 TO THE SYRIAN CRISIS. WE ARE ALL HUMAN BEINGS ON THIS EARTH.

TROLL: Does this mean I get to see her wet pussy still or nah?

SCENE ELEVEN

A year later. NICOLA and ADAM stand inside a prototype booth. They can explore the booth. Feel the walls. Let themselves imagine.

ADAM: I think this is nuts.

NICOLA: Are you joking?

ADAM: Is this wipe clean? How much did this cost?

NICOLA: It's high quality.

ADAM: How much?

NICOLA: Okay … Well nearly all –

ADAM: All?

NICOLA: We made fifty of them.

ADAM: Fifty?

NICOLA: Fucking look at it, Adam. It's amazing.

ADAM: It's not amazing. It'll tell you what it was though. It was a flat in London. It was a house in Guilford. It was Chloe's university fees. It was your university fees.

NICOLA: That's not fair, there's no way I could go to university after that.

ADAM: You could start over.

NICOLA: What the fuck do you think I'm doing? Are you getting this? Other people are gonna use these. Not me. I'm retiring. I might have to do maybe one last teeny weeny bit of promotion so we get a queue going. Just to drum up business and then before long people won't know what they're queuing for. Like Apple. And then I move into admin. I'm CEO. CEO of Protest.

ADAM: Protest?

NICOLA: Yeah. Protest. Go Pro. Test your limits. I kind of like it.

ADAM: And you think everything you just described to me is stopping?

NICOLA: What's the alternative? Lose every single penny? To have put all manner of things up my vagina for absolutely nothing?

ADAM: Nobody made you.

NICOLA: Nobody's making me now but me but what choice do I have?

ADAM: We jack this in and buy a flat and I take that job at Santander.

NICOLA: You would hate it.

ADAM: I wouldn't, actually. You'd hate it. But that's okay.
I'm not like you.

NICOLA: No.

ADAM: What?

NICOLA: No, you're just sick of sharing me with people.
And you've got it into your head that this is still sharing.

ADAM: No, Nicola, it's not about fucking sharing. It's about
sex. It's about morals. It's about … It's always about sex.
And I want it to be about us.

NICOLA: It is. I'm doing this with you.

ADAM: You're doing this in spite of me. You have a choice.

NICOLA: Look, I have to go in to come out. I have to burrow
in deep to emerge the other side. Can't you see that?
I'm successful. I'm a fucking success. I'm not leaving.

ADAM: But there'll always be something, Nic.

Pause.

Why do you never stay at mine?

NICOLA: What?

ADAM: You just … doesn't matter.

Silence.

NICOLA: Don't go to Santander. *(Beat.)* Come to Protest.

ADAM: What?

NICOLA: Come and work for me.

ADAM: Are you out of your mind?

NICOLA: No.

ADAM: I'm not a pimp.

NICOLA: Well that's handy, because I need an accountant and I'm not a prostitute.

ADAM: Of course, I meant – sorry.

NICOLA: We're a family company, we love each other and you're fucking good at numbers. It makes perfect sense. However much they've offered you, I can offer you more.

ADAM: It's not about the money.

NICOLA: I thought you'd be pleased. You'd be exec of a brand new start up. What are your course mates doing right now?

ADAM: Nic, I need to think.

NICOLA: It's as simple as this. We're gonna do this. Whether you join or not. And we're gonna make a bomb. And you'd get me. All of me. And a fuck tonne more money. *(Beat.)* Now are you in or are you in?

SCENE TWELVE

Three years later. A small conference room. Loud sofas. Very clean. Flowers. A girl, KAT, is sat on the sofa. She's very tense. CHLOE enters.

CHLOE: She'll be with you in a moment, Kat.

KAT: Alright.

CHLOE: In the meantime can I get you a tea or coffee?

KAT: Coke.

CHLOE: Hm?

KAT: Have you got a coke?

CHLOE: Yep, that's no problem, Kat. *(Beat.)* Is your partner-?

KAT: Ex-partner.

CHLOE: Oh dear. I'm so sorry. Are you on speaking terms?

KAT: No.

CHLOE: You've come to the right place, Kat. You've done all the right things. This reflects a lot worse on him than you.

KAT: Her.

CHLOE: Her. *(Beat. She passes her a tissue from a box on a side table.)* It's a nasty, horrible thing that's happened. Did you guys have one of those expensive civil wedding things?

KAT: *(Beat.)* No.

CHLOE: Dry those tears. I'll get you your coke now.

She leaves the office. KAT is left alone for a moment.

NICOLA enters.

NICOLA: Hi Kat, my name's Nicola Barker, I'm CEO of Protest.

KAT: Hi.

NICOLA: Before we start I just want to say thank you so much for coming in. I'm so glad you did. So, do you wanna tell me what's happened?

KAT: It's / in my email –

NICOLA: / In your email, yes but I'd love to hear it from you, if you don't mind? Only so I can really get a sense of what's gone on here. I'm here to listen to you today and to see how best to move forward.

KAT: Well, I … I – My girlfriend and I … My ex-girlfriend and I …

NICOLA offers up the tissue box. KAT holds up the tissue that CHLOE gave her. NICOLA nods and pops the tissue box back on the table.

Me and her made a video.

NICOLA: Okay.

KAT: It was … um … Sorry.

NICOLA: Take your time.

KAT: We made it together for our anniversary.

NICOLA: In which booth?

KAT: That one on Dean street. We got an hour.

NICOLA: And did you use any of our themes?

KAT: We …

NICOLA: There's No Judgement, here. Kat.

KAT: We used Arabian Nights.

NICOLA: Okay. *(Beat.)* Kat? You know what I'm going to say, don't you?

KAT: // No judgement.

NICOLA: // No Judgement.

KAT: Yeah. Thanks.

KAT is visibly relaxing.

It's proper nice here.

NICOLA: Well, we're a family company. Family values. It's a lovely place to work.

KAT: Seems it.

NICOLA: We're all very happy here.

KAT: Yeah?

NICOLA: So, how long was the finished edit?

KAT: Twenty minutes thirty four seconds.

NICOLA: And you used our editing suite facilities?

KAT: Yeah.

NICOLA: Fantastic. They're good aren't they?

KAT: Yeah, really –

NICOLA: And then tell me about how you discovered that this had happened, Kat.

KAT: Well … I was … browsing …

NICOLA: Just to be clear, you mean you were watching pornography?

KAT: Yeah.

NICOLA: Together?

KAT: No, by myself.

NICOLA: Okay.

KAT: And I saw something that looked familiar … I didn't expect it to be us 'coz we was private, you know? It was a smaller frame … Like, our heads had been cut off … but you can hear my voice. And she calls my name. It's us.

NICOLA: I'm so sorry, Kat.

KAT: She says it wasn't her. Can't have been, 'coz she wouldn't do something like that, but she says I done it. I reckon maybe there's something wrong with the systems or – I dunno how it works. But she reckons I done it but I would never. I love her. And now she …

NICOLA: I'm so sorry.

KAT: I told her I was coming here. To sort it. That I'd, like … sort it out and get it back. Back to private. Told her I'd get proof it wasn't me and that I'd get it taken down.

NICOLA: Right. *(Beat.)* I'm sorry your girlfriend –

KAT: Ex-girlfriend.

NICOLA: My apologies. I'm sorry that she's reacted this way. Now, you'll have had a printed contract on the day.

KAT: I got it in my bag.

NICOLA: Oh yes?

KAT pulls the document out of her bag and hands it to NICOLA. NICOLA peruses the documents. NICOLA withdraws another document from a folder.

Okay, Kat. You see here, where you pressed 'No To All Distribution'?

KAT: Yes.

NICOLA: This is a copy of your girlfr – Sorry, ex-girlfriend's contract. If you just have a look in this box here.

KAT: 'No With Sharing Rights'.

NICOLA: Right. So you two have made this video. I see that you split the cost so you both have joint ownership of this video.

KAT: Yeah.

NICOLA: And you've both ticked boxes that state that you have each read and accepted the terms and conditions before having begun your session.

KAT: Yeah.

NICOLA: Excellent. *(Beat.)* I'm so sorry, Kat.

KAT: Uh …

NICOLA: Because when you both went up to the machine in the booth to sign, you pressed 'No To All Distribution', however your girlfriend selected a different option. She has selected 'No With Sharing Rights'. Do you see?

KAT: I

NICOLA: I'll explain. Because there's different types of 'No'. We've got three options here at Protest. Number one. 'Yes To All Distribution'. You can do whatever the heck you like. Send it to anyone. Upload it anywhere.
The distribution rights also give us the power to roll it out along our subscription sites if we wanted to, which many people want. It's an enthusiastic yes. Two big thumbs up. Number two. 'No To All Distribution'. Does exactly what is says on the tin. You can't send it anywhere or share your work with anyone. Not even by text. Nothing. It's a '*No* No.' Two big thumbs down. Number three. 'No With Sharing Rights'. It means that it's yours, but you have

permission to send it among friends. You can whatsapp it,
Facebook it, Youtube it, Instagram it, Vine it – it's yours to
play with. Among friends. However, once you've shared it
among peers, what happens to it then is unfortunately out
of our hands and in the laps of whomever it's been sent to.
A Gladiator thumb. Do you see? You opted for a '*No* No'
and she's just opted for a 'No on her terms'. This is all in
the small print –

KAT: What are you saying?

NICOLA: I completely understand and this has all come as a
bit of a nasty shock.

KAT: Are you saying she done it? You're not serious?
She wouldn't –

NICOLA: Kat, I'm so sorry.

KAT: She never did it.

NICOLA: I think you're going to have to have a dialogue with
your exgirlfriend about why she would have chosen this
option and, ultimately, this outcome

KAT: But she wouldn't have done it. She can't have.

NICOLA: All the conditions are there, I'm afraid.

KAT: What does that even mean?

NICOLA: Kat, I'm trying to say that unfortunately your – she
has made a choice. She has exerted her right to that choice.
If *you* had shared this video that would be a criminal offence.
Your contract with us at Protest does not allow you to do
this. However, hers does. It could only have been her.

KAT: She would never have done this. She's moved out.
She said she couldn't be with anyone who'd do that.

NICOLA: Listen, Kat, the best course of action here is to
see if you two can make some progress in opening that
communication –

KAT: She was fumbling with the machine.

NICOLA: I'm sorry?

KAT: When we were in the booth, she was banging on the machine because she couldn't get the option she wanted. I forgot.

NICOLA: Oh really? What did she say?

KAT: She was slurring a bit, so I can't remember –

NICOLA: Slurring?

KAT: Mumbling.

NICOLA: Do you mind if I ask, I'm having a look at the time on the contract. You clocked in at the booth for 11 P.M. Had you been drinking, Kat?

KAT: I –

NICOLA: No Judgement.

KAT: *(Beat.)* We'd been out for dinner.

NICOLA: I totally get it, Kat. I do. It's only that alcohol is strictly prohibited in our booths. That is made very clear in the agreement.

KAT: I know.

NICOLA: Because then what we're discussing is a much deeper issue than distribution. Did you want to be in that booth, Kat?

KAT: Yeah, of course.

NICOLA: Did your girlfriend?

KAT: Yes.

NICOLA: But what you're implying – do correct me if I'm wrong – is that your girlfriend might have unknowingly opted for the wrong possession rights due to intoxication. Is that right?

KAT: You're saying it wrong. That's not what I mean.

NICOLA: Then what do you mean?

KAT: That it's poorly designed. The buttons are all very close together.

NICOLA: Kat, I'm really sorry this has happened to you. And I want to help you. But you've got to help me. And I think we know now that you both came to that booth having not read a vital section of the small print and slightly inebriated. Those were choices that you made. No one made you get in to the booth. Nobody forced you. Imagine that. That would be awful. We'd be shut down in seconds. Not having the choice. But you and your ex-girlfriend had the choice. And she chose to share your special moment with her friends. And somehow those friends have passed it on until now it is where it is.

KAT: But I did choose. I – I chose not to share it.

NICOLA: And you didn't. You've shared nothing. But unfortunately she has. And there's nothing we can do about that now. It's important to us that people opt for their permission rights separately. Coercion is a risk we're simply not prepared to take. We want you all to go out there and have fun. We have fun. So should you. You deserve fun. It's important.

KAT: Once it's been taken down, where do I complain? 'Coz I know she wouldn't do this.

NICOLA: Taken down?

KAT: Yeah.

NICOLA: How many websites is it currently on?

KAT: Three I think.

NICOLA: Okay. And have you tried ringing their helplines at all?

KAT: I've tried but I keep being passed on to someone else and then someone else. One website no one ever picks up.

NICOLA: Oh god, like a Kafkaesque nightmare?

KAT: But you can help.

NICOLA: Well … Here's the thing, Kat, the thing is, I really meant it earlier. The video really is yours. Yours and hers. The contracts are iron clad. My hands are somewhat tied.

KAT: Somewhat?

NICOLA: They're tied, Kat. All I can advise is you keep trying with those websites. Try and make contact with your ex-girlfriend. Try and find out what went on so you can start piecing it together for yourself.

KAT: You're not even gonna take it down?

NICOLA: The only thing left that we can do, that I'm fully prepared to do, is to reach out to your ex-girlfriend.

KAT: And do what?

NICOLA: Tell her that you have made contact with us in order to stop this and that she needs to communicate with you in order to approach these websites.

KAT: This is an absolute joke. You're not going to do anything?

NICOLA: Kat. I'm so sorry. There is nothing I can do. But please keep us updated with your progress.

KAT: You're joking.

NICOLA: Kat. I'm so sorry.

KAT: No. You do something. Do something. Get it down. Make it go.

NICOLA: I'm so sorry that your special moment is out there now. But on the plus side the pixel quality is second to none –

KAT: Excuse me?

NICOLA: Every cloud.

KAT: I don't believe this. I wanna complain.

NICOLA: You can complain to me.

KAT: Someone else. I want someone else to help me.

NICOLA: Alright. *(On an intercom.)* Gina, could you pop in for a moment, please?

KAT: Who's that?

NICOLA: Our Managing Director.

KAT: Is she gonna help me? 'Coz you just sat here and told me that my pussy's gonna be online forever and that my girlfriend's a liar.

NICOLA: Ex-girlfriend. And yes, she is.

GINA enters.

GINA: Hi there, Kat, I'm Gina Barker, Managing Director of Protest, how are you today?

KAT: I'm – I need you to –

NICOLA hands GINA a file. GINA scans it over for a while. Silence. She suddenly points out a detail to NICOLA. They look at each other.

GINA: Do you drive, Kat?

KAT: What?

GINA: Did you drive to dinner?

KAT: Who drives in central London?

GINA: Your home address here is listed as Surrey. Did you drive in? *(Beat.)* Because if we can prove that you were unfit to drive then you were legally unfit to enter into our booths. And if you were compos mentis then your ex-partner knowingly chose that option and, ultimately, this outcome.

KAT: *(Crying.)* But she wouldn't do that. She wouldn't.

NICOLA: People discover all sorts of things about their partners along the way. Aren't you glad you're finding this out about her now? Sorry for getting all tough back then. It's just so important we're all clear on where we stand and what we can and can't do.

GINA: Nicola's right I'm afraid, Kat. We've both had a look and there's nothing we can do unfortunately.

KAT: You won't help me.

NICOLA: We're helping where we can help. You need to talk to your lady.

NICOLA hands her a business card.

Now, this is my extension, okay? Do call if you have any more questions or have any progress.

GINA: Also as a gift from all of us, we have a free hour for you at a booth of your choice outside of central London. I've made it an open gift in case you didn't particularly feel like going back in one just yet, okay?

KAT: You …

GINA: It's going to be okay, Kat. You're going to be okay.

KAT takes the card and gets up shakily. She passes CHLOE, who has rushed back in slightly breathless with a bottle of coke in a plastic bag. CHLOE offers the bag to KAT. KAT exits. CHLOE drinks the coke.

NICOLA: *(To GINA.)* Thank you for that, I just knew we were going to be stuck there for ages and I've got meetings coming out of my ears. I tried everything.

GINA: It's fine. Sometimes they just need to hear it from someone else.

NICOLA: Fingers crossed I won't need you later on, but we have a few couples in, so –

CHLOE: I could be bad cop?

GINA: These are real people, Chloe.

CHLOE: Wait, wait –

NICOLA: What?

CHLOE takes the box of tissues and pulls a tissue out. She turns away, arranging it. She turns back to face NICOLA, holding the tissue over her lower face like part of a hijab.

CHLOE: *(Singing.)* 'ARABIAN NIIIIIIIIGHTS LIKE ARABIAN DAAAAAAYS'

She is belly dancing.

Too funny.

GINA: Don't.

CHLOE: I could barely keep a straight face. It's definitely in my personal top ten. I think it's fucking funny.

GINA: Chloe?

CHLOE: Yeah?

GINA: What's the company slogan?

CHLOE: … No Judgement.

GINA: No Judgement. *(Beat.)* I'd appreciate it if you at least behaved like you respected the work here.

CHLOE: I – I do, Gina, I –

GINA: Chloe, you're the highest paid teenager in the country. So if you could stop sneering in the face of the people who pay your bills, then I would greatly appreciate it. *(Beat.)* Now, we have to go. Nic's got meetings all afternoon.

CHLOE: I could do the next one for you, Nic? I could.

NICOLA: With respect, Chloe. You couldn't. *(Beat.)* Run along, now. Those tweets won't send themselves.

NICOLA and GINA exit. CHLOE blushes.

COMMENTS H

Comments.

TROLL: HOW HAS THIS DUMB BITCH WON AWARDS FOR GETTING PEOPLE TO ESSENTIALLY FUCK IN THE STREET PLEASE?

TROLL: Have you seen the speech she did when she won business woman of the year?

TROLL: BIDNESS HO OF THE YEAR LOL

TROLL: FIVE WEIRD TIPS TO LOSE BELLY FAT :)

TROLL: My mate from school used one an said it was amazing fucking plush no judgement.

TROLL: Oh my god they are incredible

TROLL: I tried to use one but the queue was massive?

TROLL: oooh the one in earls court isn't that busy usually don't use the one on southbank

TROLL: RT oooh the one in earls court isn't that busy usually don't use the one on southbank

TROLL: totally had a nap in one in the middle of the day no judgement lol

TROLL: you sir are a fucking hero

TROLL: It made me feel weird

TROLL: then get off the thread and go and watch a taylor swift video or something you cumrag jeez

TROLL: It is worrying just how much traction this is getting.

TROLL: Have you heard they're setting up booths outside London now?

TROLL: U a lier

SCENE THIRTEEN

Two weeks later. An office. Clean. Lights snap up on NICOLA, GINA, CHLOE and ADAM. They are watching a video.

GINA: How much longer is there?

NICOLA: We're not even halfway.

GINA: God. *(Beat.)* Did she register the nature of her complaint?

NICOLA: The Big C.

GINA: Fuck.

CHLOE: Yeah.

GINA: *(To NICOLA.)* Have you seen this already?

NICOLA: I cast an eye this morning but couldn't see anything 'untoward'.

CHLOE: Don't know how they've got the energy.

NICOLA: No Judgement, Chloe.

CHLOE: I know, I was –

GINA: Where was it taken?

NICOLA: Waterloo Station. The Waterloo Road exit.

CHLOE: Wait. Rewind it.

NICOLA: Why?

CHLOE: There's a –

NICOLA: What?

CHLOE: Her hand.

GINA: Where?

CHLOE: Look at her hand.

> *Pause. The video is rewound then played back. The sisters breathe a sigh of relief. CHLOE's professional anxiety is palpable.*

NICOLA: Good girl.

CHLOE: D'you reckon that'll help?

NICOLA: Help? We're laughing. Excellent spot, Chloe.

GINA: Good. *(Beat.)* Right, I've got to –

NICOLA: Go go go.

GINA: Glad that's sorted.

> *GINA exits.*

ADAM: Nicola, are you free for ten minutes?

NICOLA: No.

ADAM: Okay, how about this afternoon?

NICOLA: No, email me.

ADAM: I – okay.

ADAM exits. The awkwardness between him and NICOLA fills the room.

CHLOE: Do we need to watch the rest of it?

NICOLA: Watched it all this morning. Couldn't spot a thing either way. Good job we had your beady eye on it.

CHLOE: I'll let her know its a 'No' from us, then?

NICOLA: Go for it. She'll request a meeting anyway. They always do.

There is a woosh and the email is sent.

CHLOE: Done.

NICOLA: Cheers. *(Reading.)* Sorry … *(Searches for her name.)* Lilly. Not today, Sunshine. *(Beat.)* How many more do we have today?

CHLOE: *(Checking her phone.)* Fifty-three.

NICOLA: Mother of fuck.

CHLOE: It's fine, they're all distribution queries.

NICOLA: Don't scare me like that.

NICOLA's phone goes.

Now scram, Chlo. I'm busy. *(Beat.)* Nicola Barker of Protest speaking, No Judgement.

COMMENTS I

Comments.

TROLL: I THINK I TOTALLY SAW YOU TODAY WALKING DOWN PAST THE MCDONALDS IN OXFORD CIRCUS.

TROLL: Has anyone read the story about the homeless man they found in the Oxford Circus booth? Really sad.

TROLL: Did he make a smeg removal tutorial?

TROLL: That is horrible.

TROLL: I'm going to hide in your room tonight I have no eyes but I'll find you I slide my hand under the duvet and grab your ankle reblog to ten friends if you don't want this to happen god bless

SCENE FOURTEEN

A week later. Outside the conference room. ADAM is hovering. CHLOE walks up to the door.

ADAM: Chloe, this is a mistake. Nicola takes Big C's for a reason.

CHLOE: The fuck it's a mistake. I've read her file. I've seen Nic do it a hundred times.

ADAM: You've never done one before.

CHLOE: I actually want to climb the ladder here, Adam. Who spotted the hand?

ADAM: You, but –

CHLOE: Who spotted the hand?

ADAM: Did you watch the rest of the video?

CHLOE: I did, yeah. She's a lying whore.

ADAM: She's next door.

CHLOE: This is open shut. It'll take five minutes. Are you a pussy, Adam?

ADAM: Fuck off.

CHLOE: Are you Nicola's little bitch?

CHLOE slides in.

Hi Lilly, my name's Chloe Barker. I'm head of HR. Before we start I just want to say thank you so much for coming in today. I'm so glad you did.

ADAM is left in the hallway. He goes to leave and bumps into NICOLA.

NICOLA: Hi.

ADAM doesn't move.

Something wrong?

ADAM: No.

Pause.

Nicola?

NICOLA: What's wrong?

ADAM: I – um.

NICOLA: What?

ADAM: Nothing.

NICOLA: Just ping me an email.

ADAM: Nicola, I –

NICOLA: Adam.

ADAM: Can I take you for lunch tomorrow if you're not busy?

NICOLA: Oh for God's sake. Look, I just think that … It might be better if we didn't …

ADAM: Were you about to break up with me?

NICOLA: No. Oh God, no. *(Beat.)* No.

ADAM: I can take a lot of things, Nicola, but after everything –

NICOLA: No. All I was going to say was when we're working can we not be too lovey dovey?

ADAM: Do you want to just-?

NICOLA: At work –

ADAM: Not –

NICOLA: Just not –

ADAM: Yeah.

NICOLA: Okay?

ADAM: Okay. *(Beat.)* Well, actually. You're not going to be happy but –

NICOLA: Oh for fuck's sake, Adam, I've just been fucking clear about how I feel about personal issues being discussed at work.

ADAM: Okay.

NICOLA: Don't just lurk in the corridor waiting to pounce on me. Speak to me properly at home.

ADAM: Right.

NICOLA: Good.

CHLOE comes rushing out of the meeting room.

CHLOE: Okay, you were right I was wrong this is really difficult, she's really difficult, sorry.

She sees NICOLA.

Oh hi.

NICOLA: Who's in there?

ADAM: A Big C.

NICOLA: What the fuck? What the fuck have you done?

CHLOE: Sorry sorry sorry.

ADAM: I tried to stop her.

NICOLA: Shut up. Fuck off.

ADAM leaves.

Start talking.

CHLOE: Her name's not Lilly, it's Lolly.

NICOLA: Lolly? Like the thing you suck?

CHLOE: Rude.

NICOLA: CHLOE.

CHLOE: Sorry sorry sorry.

NICOLA: I haven't read any of the fucking documents. I needed
– A Big C, Chloe.

CHLOE: Sorry sorry sorry.

NICOLA: What's she saying happened?

CHLOE: That it was rape.

NICOLA: What do we have on her?

CHLOE: She's the hand girl. Remember? I spotted the hand
last week.

NICOLA: Right. Where's her file?

CHLOE: I left it in there.

NICOLA: You cretin.

CHLOE: I'm sorry. I thought I could – She's not how I'd
thought she'd be.

NICOLA: Is she emotional?

CHLOE: Not at all.

The moment hangs. NICOLA strides into the conference room.

SCENE FIFTEEN

We're in the room with NICOLA and KAT, who is calling herself LOLLY.

NICOLA: Hi, Lilly, I'm –

KAT: Lolly. It's Lolly.

NICOLA: Of course. I'm so sorry, Lolly, for some reason our system had you down as Lilly.

KAT: I guess I'm lots of things. On your system.

NICOLA: Right. Well, Lolly, it's lovely to meet you.

KAT: Is it though?

NICOLA: *(Beat.)* Of course. I'm Nicola Barker, CEO of Protest.

KAT: I know who you are.

NICOLA: Right. *(Beat.)* Please sit down.

    LOLLY is already sat down. Beat.

    I understand you've been talking to my colleague.

KAT: Your sister.

NICOLA: Excuse me?

KAT: She's your sister.

NICOLA: Yes. Yes, she is. We make no secret of that. We're a family business.

KAT: Then why did you say 'colleague' like it was filth?

NICOLA: *(Beat.)* I don't think I –

KAT: I get you.

NICOLA: I beg your pardon?

KAT: Fobbing me off with your sis.

NICOLA: I –

KAT: What do you call her? I've seen it on those youtube clips. Those interviews. What do you call her?

NICOLA: If we could talk –

KAT: Chlo. That's it. 'Chlo'.

Pause.

NICOLA: If we could discuss why you're here today, Lolly, I'd really appreciate that.

KAT: *(Shrugging.)* I got raped in one of your booths. Figured you'd sort it.

NICOLA: Okay. Now, I understand that what happened to you is an extremely delicate and serious matter –

KAT: Delicate.

NICOLA: Pardon?

KAT: You've watched it? Delicate isn't the word.

NICOLA: *(Beat.)* Lolly, I'd like to speak for a moment if that's alright? Okay?

KAT: Sure.

NICOLA: Thank you. Now I am fully aware that this is an extremely serious allegation and one that requires thorough investigation. How it works here is that in order for a claim to be considered for investigation we expect you to have reported the crime to the police and for them to have gathered enough evidence for a claim to be pursued –

KAT: I've done that.

NICOLA: Thank you. Thank you for that. *(Beat.)* Having done that and with the police's approval of sufficient evidence we then ask you to approach us in order to investigate the claim.

KAT: I've / done that

NICOLA: / done that, yes you have. And we're grateful.
So grateful you did. *(Beat.)* I watched your tape, Lolly.
I watched it twice.

KAT: Turn you on?

Silence.

NICOLA: I don't think that's appropriate in the wake of what
we're discussing.

KAT: Sorry. It was a joke.

NICOLA: *(Beat.)* Lolly, I'm going to cut to the chase, okay?
I'm sure you'd appreciate that.

LOLLY shrugs.

We've reviewed the footage and I'm afraid we don't think
you have a claim here. To us the acts performed in the
booth are consensual. At no point do you withdraw your
consent throughout the duration. There is no physical
force employed, or indeed, force with regards to opting for
possession rights. As far as I can see, this was a consensual
encounter which has gone awry. The conditions just aren't
there. What would you say to that, Lolly?

KAT: *(Pause.)* I'd say that I got raped and you're fucking this up.

NICOLA: I don't appreciate that language when I'm trying to
help –

KAT: You're only trying to help yourself.

NICOLA: I don't think that's fair.

KAT: I was threatened.

NICOLA: By what means, Lolly?

KAT: He threatened me … He blackmailed me.

NICOLA: By what means, Lolly?

KAT: Before we go in. He threatens me.

NICOLA: I can't help what happens outside of the booth, Lolly. I can only take responsibility for what happens inside and at no point do you raise the alarm.

KAT: How could I when he'd threatened me?

NICOLA: There were plenty of things you could have done or shouted, Lolly.

KAT: Stop saying my name.

NICOLA: I'm sorry –

KAT: You're not. Stop it. You're saying it wrong.

NICOLA: … Lolly?

KAT: Fuck off.

NICOLA: *(Beat.)* Lolly, we treat consent claims extremely seriously. We have a name for them here. We call them the 'The Big C'. Because as far as we're concerned these are just as life destroying as cancer. We have a duty to respect and investigate every single claim. And we do. We have investigated yours and been unable to find any evidence of wrong doing.

KAT: The police said they won't be able to press unless you agree.

NICOLA: And we won't be agreeing, unfortunately.

KAT: I don't get why.

NICOLA: Out of interest, have you watched the video?

KAT: Yeah. 'Course I have.

NICOLA: Would you be willing to watch a segment of footage with me? No Judgement, of course.

KAT: …

NICOLA: I was wondering if you might be able to describe to me what's happening here.

NICOLA takes a remote control, selects the video, and presses play. We hear sex noises. KAT looks uncomfortable.

There. Can you tell me what happens? Right there. What are you doing there?

KAT: I – I take his hand.

NICOLA: And?

KAT: I make it hold me.

NICOLA: Where?

KAT: My arse.

NICOLA: Right. Then?

KAT: Then?

NICOLA: What happens to your hand after that?

KAT: I … It stays on my arse.

NICOLA: And where's his hand?

KAT: Underneath … my hand.

NICOLA: Underneath, that's right, Lolly. It stays underneath your hand. You take your hand. Find his with your own. Place it on your bottom and then keep it there with your hand. And there it stays.

KAT: But –

NICOLA: I'm afraid that's a move that firmly classifies the content as consensual.

KAT: He said I had to.

NICOLA: I'm afraid without proof of coercion that's not up for debate. It's really your word against his on this one. And as far as this video goes, you two seem a very happy, sexually active couple. The sex looks healthy, albeit a little rough, but there's No Judgement here.

KAT: I didn't want to.

NICOLA: Did you say No?

KAT: I – I went unwillingly.

NICOLA: Did the word 'No' leave your mouth?

KAT: No.

NICOLA: But you're still insisting this wasn't consensual?

KAT: I didn't want to. I made it clear.

NICOLA: How? Because the word 'No' is the all important classification that myself, the police and indeed your sexual partners are going to be looking for. 'No' is the word. And its an enthusiastic 'NO' we need rather than a 'No'? Or a 'nah' or even a 'mm'. Do you understand? *(Beat.)* Yes or no?

KAT: I've seen your first tape.

Silence.

NICOLA: Excuse me?

KAT: I've seen your first tape. The one in Ibiza.

NICOLA: *(Beat.)* I don't see that that has anything to do with –

KAT: You look terrified.

NICOLA: …

KAT: That bit where one of the guys hits you round the face with his cock. Where he hits you. And it makes that slap sound, you look down the camera for, like, a second. And you can sit here and say you loved it. But your eyes look like a cow. Like a cow just before it gets killed. For beef. Like it knows its going to die.

NICOLA: *(Beat.)* Have you ever seen a cow just before it gets killed?

KAT: Nah.

NICOLA: Then I'd appreciate you not using metaphors to describe my body of work that appear to be beyond your understanding.

Pause.

Are we done, Lolly?

KAT: You think that because someone did this to you, you can do it to everyone else?

NICOLA: *(On an intercom.)* Chloe, could you send security please?

KAT: You don't have security. It's just 'Chlo'. And I wouldn't waste my energy trying to hurt you. You're hurting yourself.

NICOLA: Lolly, I think we're done here. This meeting is over.

KAT: Must be fun up in your little castle playing with all this money and power and sex and fucking over women calling people liars. You're not like any feminist I've ever met.

NICOLA: Goodbye, Lolly.

KAT: You shouldn't've fucked me. You're gonna get fucked.

LOLLY gets up and leaves. She passes CHLOE and ADAM on the way out who are responding to the intercom.

She didn't even recognise me.

COMMENTS J

Comments.

TROLL: That's horrible.

TROLL: Also the whole 'no' thing is fucking sketchy.

TROLL: I just don't like the way it's not even called into question at all. Like it's shut down before it's begun.

TROLL: It's her voice that gets me. Urgh.

TROLL: nicola barker is only good for blowing me tbh

TROLL: Nicola Barker is a moron.

TROLL: Who is the chick who fucked in the booth and is she dtf?

SCENE SIXTEEN

A day later. The three sisters are back in the office. CHLOE's phone continues to buzz throughout the scene. CHLOE is engaged in the scene but constantly checking her phone.

GINA: Start talking.

CHLOE: Well, we all watched her video … Um … Then she requested a meeting after we denied her claim. She, um … had the meeting –

GINA: With you?

CHLOE: Uh … Yeah. Yeah with me.

GINA: Was there any particular reason that she had the meeting with you and not with Nicola?

CHLOE: I … Er … No.

NICOLA: I'm the face of the company.

CHLOE: I know.

NICOLA: We agreed this early on, it is crucial Big C's see me. I'm the living breathing face. People know me. I'm the faith. I'm the trust. I'm Big Brother. I'm Putin. I'm Che Guevara.

GINA: Then what happened.

CHLOE: She said she wanted to speak to Nicola. That she knew I wasn't meant to take the meeting … She seemed to know …

GINA: Well of course she knew. She'd been in before.

CHLOE: I saw the hand.

GINA: What?

CHLOE: The hand. In the video, I saw –

GINA: Do you want a fucking medal?

CHLOE: *(Beat.)* But I still –

GINA: Oh for crying out loud, there's enough of us. Monkeys. Shakespeare. Typewriters.

CHLOE's phone buzzes once more.

FOR FUCK'S SAKE, CHLOE.

CHLOE: I can't turn it off, Gina, it's all the tweets. We need to know what's happening. I'm trying to –

GINA: What was she in for before? Kat? Or Lolly? What's her real name? Anyone?

CHLOE: Kat. Her real name's Kat.

NICOLA: She came in for a distribution enquiry three weeks ago.

GINA: And neither of you recognised her?

CHLOE: Distribution enquiries have shot up, Gina, there are too many, we can't keep up. You didn't recognise her either. We all watched her video. You were there too.

GINA: I met her for less than a minute. You both had meetings with her. It is your job to remember.

CHLOE's phone buzzes again.

CHLOE: Fuck.

GINA: What?

CHLOE: This isn't good. '@nicolaprotests haven't you got dicks to suck instead of terrorising vulnerable women? #norestforprotest'. I don't understand how Alex Campbell used to be so nice and now she's such a cunt.

ADAM enters on his phone.

ADAM: Sorry, Alex, if you could hold on one moment – just – I've got Vice on the phone here. They want to know how the fuck that rape video is trending?

NICOLA: Trending?

CHLOE: Hang on, they're coming in too fast for me to – oh fuck. He's right.

NICOLA: No.

They crowd round CHLOE's phone.

GINA: How has this happened?

NICOLA: What did she select?

CHLOE: 'No With Sharing Rights'.

NICOLA: No.

CHLOE: She did.

NICOLA: Fuck.

GINA: What?

NICOLA: I'm just – Fuck.

ADAM: What do I tell them, Gina?

NICOLA: Say that she must have shared it herself. She has to have done.

ADAM: But they're saying she shared it with them and absolutely no one else and it wasn't them.

NICOLA: Then tell them she's a lying money grabbing whore and that her and Alex Campbell deserve one another.

ADAM: *(Beat.)* Hi there. Listen, we can confirm 100% that the video didn't leak through us. Our contracts are iron clad, they –

Right. Well, of course we'll co-operate with –

She's hung up.

CHLOE: I mean who has actual pretend rape sex because someone was mean to them?

GINA: Thank you, Chloe. You may go.

CHLOE: I'm really sorry.

GINA: GET OUT, CHLOE.

CHLOE leaves. The girls lock horns. ADAM looks uncomfortable.

NICOLA: Gina –

GINA: How on earth didn't you spot it? From the way that girl behaved. It was a trap, Nicola. I mean the girl's gay for christ's sake. It was staring you in the face. She selected 'No With Sharing Rights'. She wanted to share it.

NICOLA: But I didn't know that, Gina. I had no fucking idea. If Chloe hadn't fucked it up

GINA: Chloe isn't your problem right now. Do you have any idea how much trouble we're in?

NICOLA: …

GINA: Adam, read her the Vice article. The headline. *(Beat.)* Now, please.

He gets his phone and gets the article up.

ADAM: 'RAPE VICTIMS SHOWN FOOTAGE OF THEIR OWN RAPES: WELCOME TO THE MURKY UNDERWORLD OF PROTEST'

Pause.

GINA: We're ruined, Nic.

NICOLA: We're not ruined. This is a blip. We're gonna win this.

GINA: I need time to think about where we go from here.

ADAM: I think we should call an internal investigation.

GINA: That's the first sensible thing someone's said.

NICOLA: What? I don't think that's helpful.

GINA: Well, I agree with Adam.

NICOLA: Don't do an internal – there's no need to – A press conference.

GINA: What?

NICOLA: I'll do a press conference.

GINA: We will get eaten alive.

NICOLA: That's what people want. They don't want a cold hard report. They want the face. Bring it back to sisters. Bring it back to – Put me on a panel and I can talk. I can do it. Just watch me.

Pause.

GINA: Okay. *(To ADAM.)* Can you get everything together? We're going to have to over-prepare.

GINA leaves, exhausted.

NICOLA: What?

ADAM: Footage, Nicola.

NICOLA: Because when you show them the footage they back down. It always works. It proves they're lying. It proves they want money.

ADAM: What about the ones that weren't lying?

NICOLA: We've had zero convictions. That means zero rapes.

ADAM leaves. NICOLA hits herself gently.

COMMENTS K

Comments.

TROLL: SHE IS DISGUSTING

TROLL: Can't believe she let herself get raped to prove a point

TROLL: she didn't get raped she had organised consensual sex to prove a point

TROLL: lol dat crazy

TROLL: isn't she a lesbian? And if so do u reckon she's cured now?

TROLL: that is a horrible disgusting thing to say and is incredibly hurtful to the LGBT community

TROLL: the fact is she took the d to get back at someone who took the d time for everyone to chill the fuk out and let the whores squabble amongst themselves

TROLL: lol tho anyone notice how the dyke had a hairy minge in her first video and shaved in her second?

TROLL: isn't it interesting that even tho she a dyke she know exactly what to do with a dick. Hmm. #notalesbianjustuntrained

SCENE SEVENTEEN

Three days later. The three sisters sit down to a panel.

NICOLA: Thank you all for coming today. I'm gonna jump right in. We all feel horrified by the recent events here at Protest. It has racked us all. My sisters and I want to take this opportunity to extend our deepest sympathies to the woman in question after the way she was interrogated. Woman in question – Kat. Her name is Kat. And she isn't anonymous because you all know her name from her article. In this instance we have been fortunate. Kat Lewis was not attacked. She merely posed as a victim. A victim called Lolly. Kat felt that she had been poorly treated by us on her first visit and went to extreme lengths to seek some sort of personal closure. Her determination is almost commendable and not to be sniffed at. The consequences of her actions have highlighted a wider risk to us here at Protest. One that we take very seriously indeed. Abuse goes on. Everywhere. For every Kat Lewis, there's a Lolly. These booths are about people. And I refuse to hide behind business jargon when ours is a company that brings people into physical contact with one another. The purest form of contact there is. We are also running #HerNameIsLolly for victims of abuse and have set up a helpline for all those who feel affected by this event. We are aware of our responsibility to the wider public. Know that if you or anyone you know has been affected you are not a number. You are not a statistic. You are a person.

CHLOE: Follow #HerNameIsLolly for more.

GINA: We can confirm that we are currently in the process of remanufacturing our booths to make sure that our consumers feel completely safe at all times.

NICOLA: We've tripled security to triple your pleasure. Now that's said and done, I'd like to open the floor for questions. Let's talk about sex.

Laughter.

JOURNALIST: Matt Hooper, Independent –

NICOLA: Hi there, Matt.

JOURNALIST: Er – Hi. Um, what changes will you be making to your external investigation system?

NICOLA: That's a great question.

GINA: We've introduced a CPS – a consumer personal statement. This is our consumers way of expressing how they feel regardless of the outcome of their claim. It's their voice.

NICOLA: It gives the enquiry a less 'corporate' feel. More bedroom less boardroom.

JOURNALIST: Susie Watkins, Marie Claire.

NICOLA: Hi, Susie. Fab dress.

JOURNALIST: Thank you. So how are these new booths going to look?

NICOLA: Ace question, Susie. Well, as well as new interiors –

CHLOE: – leopard print –

NICOLA: – the sexiest thing we can guarantee is absolute safety.

GINA: We're doubling our camera coverage so not only doubling potential evidence but also getting the most out of your Protest session with better angles.

NICOLA: It's a win win for everyone, am I right ladies?

JOURNALIST: Hi, Alex Campbell, Vice.

NICOLA: *(Beat.)* Hi, Alex.

JOURNALIST: Hi. How are you able to justify your treatment of Kat Lewis after having been on the receiving end of the same treatment yourself?

GINA: That's not –

NICOLA: It's cool, Geen. The answer's quite simple really. I have no trouble justifying anything because the same thing didn't happen to me. We are forgetting that Kat Lewis arrived at the Protest headquarters posing as someone else claiming to have been raped so –

JOURNALIST: I meant more in terms of being slutshamed.

GINA: That's not an appropriate question.

NICOLA: I don't consider myself a victim of slutshaming. And neither does Kat Lewis, I'm sure, considering she was also a willing consumer who engaged in consensual sex. Any more?

TROLL: Get your tits out.

GINA: This is a press conference.

NICOLA: It's alright, Geen. We're naturally protective of one another. That's what being sisters is all about. So. Get my tits out. I think someone's forgotten just how sexy consent is, hey? Can't keep it in your pants? Why not make me a video in one of our booths and upload it to our channels? I look forward to it, mister.

Laughter.

TROLL: How do you sleep at night?

GINA: How about we hear from some grown ups.

JOURNALIST: I have another.

NICOLA: Hi again, Alex.

JOURNALIST: When Protest launched early last year you spoke at the event about how one of your company aims was to tackle the stigma of revenge pornography by saturating the market.

NICOLA: That's right I did.

JOURNALIST: I just want to ask if you feel you've achieved this goal considering you're selling Protest videos on to third party buyers for profit?

Silence. NICOLA's smile flickers.

GINA: I don't understand the question.

JOURNALIST: Nicola Barker has been selling on videos made in her booths to the Pornhub network for a profit. My question is, Nicola, if you feel you've-?

GINA: This is an allegation that is entirely unfounded. We can assure you all that this is not the case.

JOURNALIST: I've been made aware of documents drawn up by yourself, Nicola, that were signed off on by an Adam Brewer, authorising the sale of thousands of consumer videos. Your booth users who selected 'No With Sharing Rights'. I just wanted to hear from the lady herself.

Silence. CHLOE and GINA look at NICOLA. NICOLA doesn't break eye contact with the journalist. She is frozen with a smile on her face.

CHLOE: Fuck.

NICOLA hits herself gently. Maybe we don't notice. She picks up her glass of water and drains it. She gets up to go.

NICOLA: Excuse me, one moment.

GINA: *(Grabbing NICOLA by the wrist.)* You go nowhere.

Silence.

NICOLA: Okay. I have a question for you. My turn. How do I win? Because as wonderful as this all is, I'd love to know how I can fucking win. Can anyone tell me? Anyone at all?

Pause.

Come on then. Who wants me? Come and get me.

A camera flashes.

SCENE EIGHTEEN

Later that evening. NICOLA hurriedly packing up her things. ADAM enters.

ADAM: Where the fuck do you think you're going?

NICOLA: You can't tell me what to do.

ADAM: You're not going anywhere until you clear my name.

NICOLA: You just humiliated me live.

ADAM: Nicola, you forged my fucking signature.

NICOLA: I need Protest to be a success. I didn't have a choice.

ADAM: Of course you had a choice. You had too much fucking choice.

NICOLA: I couldn't lose it.

ADAM: Do you realise that I can't ever work again now? That my name will always be associated with fraud. If I hadn't …

NICOLA: If you hadn't what, Adam? At least be man enough to fucking say it. If you hadn't leaked our accounts. Why the fuck didn't you tell me you knew?

ADAM: Oh let's see, because you repeatedly ignore me at work, at home, in bed –

NICOLA: Fuck you.

ADAM: If I had written it across my face and laid down in front of your office you'd have fucking stepped over me. I gave up a job to come here. A great job.

NICOLA: You did it because you were scared to lose me.

ADAM: This is cruel, Nicola.

NICOLA: What? Crueler than letting me get eaten alive out there and ruining everything I've worked for? Go fuck yourself.

ADAM: That's what I do anyway, 'coz we haven't fucked in a year.

NICOLA: Just fuck off, Adam. I'm not going to let you piss over everything I've worked for.

ADAM: What you have done is illegal. You have exploited thousands of people. You used my name. You took our company ethos and raped it.

NICOLA: *My* company.

ADAM: You'll go to prison.

NICOLA: I won't.

ADAM: You will. It's fraud. You're going to lose everything. Everything. Your family. Your mum has fucking shares in the company, Nicola.

NICOLA: I'm losing nothing.

ADAM: I'm going to press charges.

NICOLA: You wouldn't.

ADAM: See you there.

NICOLA: I'm Nicola Barker.

ADAM: You stopped being Nicola Barker in a nightclub six years ago.

NICOLA: You weren't there.

ADAM: You could have come to me.

NICOLA: You weren't in Ibiza.

ADAM: How can anyone ever help you, Nicola, when you don't let them?

NICOLA: You called me disgusting.

ADAM: You broke my fucking heart.

NICOLA: You wanted to hit me.

ADAM: I wanted to marry you.

NICOLA: No one understood.

ADAM: If you were bored then you should have broken up with me instead of ruining my fucking life.

NICOLA: What about my life? I just want to live.

ADAM: You're not dying, Nicola. Why do you live as though you're dying? I have tried so hard. I have spent years pleading on my knees. I tried. I am trying. I don't understand.

NICOLA: You can't understand because you don't know the meaning of shame. Because you could get sucked off on a dance floor with twenty other men and then walk off into the night and never fucking think twice about it and get that job at Santander and take that girl in HR out for coffee and date her and marry her and love her and never fucking stop to think about telling her what you did. Because you didn't do anything, right? You don't know shame. Or maybe, now you do.

ADAM: I'm never asleep. *(Beat.)* When you masturbate at night and you think I'm asleep. I'm not asleep. So don't say I don't know shame.

NICOLA tries to leave. ADAM blocks her path.

No, you don't.

NICOLA: Get out of my way.

ADAM: You do something. You write something or –

ADAM gets his phone out and presses record.

Tell people what you've done. Tell everyone I didn't do it.

GINA enters. She has been crying. Pause. ADAM lowers his phone.

ADAM: *(Beat.)* I wish I'd never met any of you.

He leaves without looking at NICOLA.

GINA: I don't blame him. I actually think it's what you deserve.

NICOLA: Really?

GINA: I think that this has spiralled completely out of control and that that was the only way you'd learn.

NICOLA: Did I need to be taught a lesson, Gina?

GINA: Nicola, you broke the law. You breached contracts that have ruined thousands of lives. What you've done is disgusting.

NICOLA: I did what I had to do to save it.

GINA: You should have told me.

NICOLA: Why? You'd have judged me. You hate this. You hate sex. You hate men. You hate yourself. You hate me.

GINA: That's not true.

NICOLA: You can't bear it. Any of it. Are you a virgin, Gina? Is that why you think this is disgusting?

GINA: You're disgusting. The things you're saying are disgusting.

NICOLA: I'm not disgusting. I'm not. You are. You were looking for an excuse to shut this whole thing down and now you've got it. Well done, Adam. Well done, you.

GINA: I've given up my whole fucking life trying to pull you out of danger, Nicola.

NICOLA: Oh please, you're in your twenties.

GINA: My twenties have revolved entirely around you.

NICOLA: Then you should have gone and got some then instead living through me.

GINA: I could hit you.

NICOLA: So hit me.

GINA: …

NICOLA: I thought so. You've always been a pussy.

GINA: *(Beat.)* I think I'm leaving now. *(Beat.)* I'm done. Chloe and I are done now. Mum's done. Adam's done. We're all done now.

NICOLA: …

GINA: You're my sister. And I'm trying to love you. *(Beat.)* But I wish you'd never been born.

NICOLA: …

GINA: I didn't mean that. I didn't. I just … I wish it was how it was. I wish none of this had ever happened. If we'd done something. If we'd gone to the police. None of this –

NICOLA: I did go to the police.

Pause.

GINA: What?

NICOLA: I'd already been to the police.

Silence.

GINA: *(Beat.)* Why didn't you tell me?

NICOLA: *(Beat.)* They wouldn't press charges until he uploaded it. They weren't going to help me. You couldn't help me. So I uploaded it before he could. I thought you could help me. But you thought I was a dirty horrible slut.

GINA slaps NICOLA. Pause. CHLOE enters. Silence. GINA is appalled at herself. She leaves in tears. CHLOE stares at NICOLA. NICOLA hits herself.

Sorry Chloe.

SCENE NINETEEN

NICOLA is in a police station. There is a POLICEMAN and a POLICEWOMAN.

POLICEMAN: So you're saying he –

NICOLA: I didn't know it was being taken.

POLICEMAN: Yeah.

NICOLA: And now I'm being –

POLICEMAN: And this is to cause distress?

NICOLA: I'm sorry?

POLICEMAN: I'm asking if this is intended to cause distress.

NICOLA: I don't know … I don't know if you're joking.

POLICEMAN: We wouldn't joke about something like this.

NICOLA: Yes. Yes, this is explicitly intended to cause distress.

POLICEMAN: Because you're telling us he wants to post it on the website of the club he manages, is that correct?

NICOLA: Yes.

POLICEMAN: Because, the thing is, and I'm just trying to show you how they'd pick holes, you see, if it's that … er … that kind of club, for want of a better expression, then this could be serving as promotional material.

NICOLA: It's not that kind of club.

POLICEMAN: It's not?

NICOLA: It's a standard club in Ibiza.

POLICEMAN: Oh. *(Beat.)* Right.

Pause. The police look at one another.

POLICEMAN: We're not doubting that this is horrible for you, Nicola, okay? This is a frightening upsetting experience for you and we don't doubt that for a minute, do we Helen?

POLICEWOMAN: No.

NICOLA: Okay.

POLICEMAN: Okay. Now the thing is he hasn't actually posted this video anywhere yet, has he?

NICOLA: No, but –

POLICEMAN: Well, the thing is he hasn't actually committed a crime yet.

NICOLA: I –

POLICEWOMAN: He's abroad too, isn't he?

POLICEMAN: Well, yeah, that's another kettle of fish.

NICOLA: Why does that matter?

POLICEWOMAN: Well, we're in the UK, aren't we?

NICOLA: I'm aware.

POLICEMAN: But the crime happened abroad.

POLICEWOMAN: And if he's still abroad / well

POLICEMAN: / well we're going to have to talk to their local police force and try and ascertain –

NICOLA: But they won't do anything.

POLICEMAN: Have you contacted them out there?

NICOLA: I … No.

POLICEWOMAN: Why not?

NICOLA: Well, I came to you. I came here. To you guys. Because, I –

POLICEMAN: I think I understand.

NICOLA: I don't think you do.

POLICEMAN: Okay, Nicola. I'm going to ask you a question now that may be a difficult question to answer.

NICOLA: Okay.

POLICEMAN: Did you want that sexual act to happen?

NICOLA: I –

POLICEMAN: Did you want that to happen to you?

POLICEWOMAN: Was it enjoyable?

POLICEMAN: I don't think we can ask / that

POLICEWOMAN: / What we're asking is if this was your decision. Did you instigate this?

NICOLA: I didn't instigate it.

POLICEMAN: That's not –

NICOLA: Did I want it?

POLICEMAN: // No.

POLICEWOMAN: // Yes.

Beat. The police look at one another.

POLICEMAN: That's not quite –

POLICEWOMAN: You weren't forced or pressured to do this?

NICOLA: No.

Pause. The police look at one another.

POLICEMAN: Okay. *(Beat.)* That's great.

Silence.

Alrighty. Now, Nicola, this is the difficult bit. I totally appreciate this won't be what you're wanting to hear.

NICOLA: You're not going to do anything?

POLICEMAN: Now, that's not what we've said, is it? No. What we're saying is that, unfortunately, we kind of need to wait until he posts the video before we can take action.

NICOLA: I was filmed without my consent.

POLICEMAN: If this was blackmail then that would be different. We're not currently dealing with blackmail. We're currently dealing with a – a revenge –

POLICEWOMAN: And even if it was we wouldn't advise you pay.

97

POLICEMAN: Well. Helen's right in that – Well what tends to happen –

POLICEWOMAN: Once people pay it can often lead to perpetrators pressuring victims for more money and after all that they tend to post it anyway.

POLICEMAN: What Helen means is that it's often hard to –

NICOLA: I want to press charges. I –

POLICEWOMAN: You look down the camera.

NICOLA: Excuse me?

POLICEWOMAN: You look down the camera. And you're smiling. *(Beat.)* I'm only bringing this up because this is what would be used against you in court.

NICOLA: …

POLICEWOMAN: We're just trying to do our job, Nicola. And I think you're going to have a hard time defending this.

NICOLA: I don't understand why.

POLICEWOMAN: *(Beat.)* Because all the conditions are there, I'm afraid.

NICOLA: What does that even mean? Does that mean I don't look vulnerable enough?

POLICEWOMAN: // Yes.

POLICEMAN: // I … Let's just wait and see what he does, okay?

The sounds of the Ibiza swell.

SCENE TWENTY

NICOLA is drunk. We are in Ibiza. The PROMOTER is pouring her a drink.

PROMOTER: You look like Bambi.

NICOLA: Yeah?

PROMOTER: That can be your name.

NICOLA: Bambi?

PROMOTER: You don't like it?

NICOLA: A little tacky.

NICOLA laughs.

PROMOTER: Tacky? You wanna talk about tacky. After that, my love? After what you just did? You're funny.

NICOLA: Thanks.

PROMOTER: A girl who can take a compliment. *(He hands her the drink.)* Don't meet many of them, hey?

NICOLA: Guess not.

Silence. They are staring at one another.

I'm awesome.

PROMOTER: No, darling, *that* was awesome.

NICOLA: I'm awesome.

PROMOTER: You're okay.

NICOLA: I'm awesome.

PROMOTER: *(Laughing.)* You're a funny one.

NICOLA: I know.

PROMOTER: *(Beat.)* I'll have you back next year, you know.

NICOLA: Oh yeah?

PROMOTER: If you want. You're a good rep. You've been good with the young people. They like you.

NICOLA: That's because I'm a young person.

PROMOTER: Ha.

NICOLA: And a lot of people love me.

PROMOTER: You love yourself.

NICOLA: I do.

PROMOTER: How come?

NICOLA: Huh?

PROMOTER: How come you love yourself?

NICOLA: I don't need to give you a reason.

PROMOTER: I wasn't saying it's a bad thing, girl.

NICOLA: You were a bit.

PROMOTER: I wasn't. I swear. *(Beat.)* Has anyone ever told you you've got beautiful eyes?

NICOLA suddenly starts laughing.

What?

NICOLA: Of course you'll bloody have me back next year.

PROMOTER: What you saying?

NICOLA: You just said that you'll have me back this year?

PROMOTER: Next year.

NICOLA: Oh yeah.

PROMOTER: This year is this year, you little pisshead.

NICOLA: Right.

PROMOTER: Next year.

NICOLA: Next year.

PROMOTER: What about it?

NICOLA: Well of course you'll bloody have me back. After that.

PROMOTER: Ha. Yeah. You wanna get back out there. *(Beat.)* You could work in a strip club.

NICOLA: Ha. Not a shitty club like this one.

PROMOTER: A shitty club, hey?

NICOLA: No, no, I'm teasing. It's great.

PROMOTER: But you could, you know. *(Beat.)* That was good.

NICOLA: Yeah?

PROMOTER: *(Beat.)* I'm good.

NICOLA: Oh yeah? Back in the day?

PROMOTER: No, you bitch. Now. I'm good now.

NICOLA: *(Laughing.)* Sorry. But you're not though, are you?

PROMOTER: I am. I fucking am.

NICOLA: You're funny.

PROMOTER: You're the funny one, Miss Bitch.

> *He goes to tickle her and she bats him away. He grabs her wrist. He holds it for too long.*

PROMOTER: Come on, let me show you something sexy.

NICOLA: Don't ruin things by getting your dick out.

> *The PROMOTER goes up to her. He crouches down beside her. NICOLA hesitates. The moment hangs.*

PROMOTER: Who said anything about my dick?

> *Then he gets his phone out. He presses play.*

Look at you, Miss Bambi.

NICOLA: You filmed it?

PROMOTER: Yeah?

NICOLA: What the fuck?

PROMOTER: You look fantastic.

NICOLA: I –

PROMOTER: You're beautiful.

NICOLA: You –

PROMOTER: You're so beautiful.

NICOLA: Delete it.

PROMOTER: Come on now we can enjoy your beautiful work, hey?

NICOLA: Delete it now.

PROMOTER: Not such a funny girl now. Where's your sense of humour? Gone on holiday? *(He laughs.)*

NICOLA: I'm serious, delete it.

PROMOTER: I can't.

NICOLA: Why the fuck not? You have to.

PROMOTER: I don't want to.

NICOLA: Please. Please delete it. I'm begging you, delete it.

PROMOTER: I need to keep it.

NICOLA: Why?

PROMOTER: For me. When I masturbate.

NICOLA: That's disgusting.

PROMOTER: No, beautiful girl. What you just did was disgusting. It was disgusting.

He begins stroking her cheek.

Twenty minutes ago you let all those men put their dicks in you, hey. In your mouth and round your face, and you feel all full now? And you arched your back like a little pussy cat and stick your tongue out for more, hmm? I want you, funny girl. You're good and I'm good. Let's be good to each other, hey? You do it for them and now you do it for me. Because we're good.

He goes to kiss NICOLA but she jerks her head away. He holds her face.

(Pause.) You're disgusting. *(Pause.)* I love you.

He tries to kiss her again but this time she reaches for the phone. He holds it out of reach.

Naughty girl.

NICOLA shoves him hard.

NICOLA: Get the fuck off me. You're disgusting.

PROMOTER: No, you are. You're a little bitch.

NICOLA shoves him again.

You're a foul, diseased, ugly pussy bitch.

NICOLA: I'm not gonna fuck you. Why the fuck would I fuck you?

PROMOTER: You're a cunt.

NICOLA: No, I *have* a cunt. And it's amazing. And you can't have it.

NICOLA doubles over laughing.

PROMOTER: Cunt. Why are you laughing at me? Hey? What have I done to make you laugh at me? I don't deserve it. It's not nice. You're a bitch. You're a cunt.

NICOLA shakes her head laughing at him. She wobbles a bit and heads towards the exit.

Fuck off. What, you're gonna go crying, telling everyone that I touched you? Nobody'll believe you. Girls like you. Whores like you. You can get on a plane tomorrow, you ugly slut. You get on a plane and fuck off home. Nobody's gonna want you here when I'm done with this. Teasing me all summer. You and your disgusting pussy. Go back to England and go fuck everyone there with your rotten pussy. There's other girls out there now in the bar. Right now. Nobody gives a fuck about you. There are more girls. Do you understand? You aren't special. There are more girls who fuck better than you.

NICOLA goes to leave.

Where the fuck do you think you're going?

NICOLA: You can't tell me what to do.

PROMOTER: Yes, I can. I have you.

NICOLA: Nobody has me. Watch me.

Acknowledgements

This would never have come off the ground without Lisa Cagnacci, Steve Harper, Paul Robinson and all at 503 – thank you all so very much for your continued support and for letting me spill another idea out of my head and onto your stage.

A big fat thank you to Jessica Campbell, Jack Sain, Tom Bailey, Frances Bradshaw, the Clickbait Team, all at D.E.M. and Fools & Kings. Thank you all for being wonderful, mad and ambitious and for making the play what it is.

A huge thank you also to Jules Haworth and Deirdre O'Halloran and everyone at Soho Theatre for all their support and feedback when the play was in its early stages.

Thanks to Giles Smart, Jennifer Thomas, Charlotte Davies and all at United Agents. You are a dream team.

To Mum, Dad, Lucy, Flora and Ella – You are incredible people. thank you the enormous support. For being there. For understanding and for trying to understand when you couldn't. That alone means the world. And I promise to wear smart shoes on press night.

To Deborah and Jess. Our Hurly Burlys and fish suppers made this possible. Thank you.

To Chandan. Without your shoulder to lean on this play would not exist. A hun of the highest order.

To Holly. You nurtured this from it being a thought in my head to where it is now. You are an astonishing human being. Thank you for your unwavering faith, hard work and friendship. Thank you.